Discipline with care

Applying biblical correction in your church

Stephen McQuoid

©Day One Publications 2008
First printed 2008

A CIP record is held at the British Library

ISBN 978-1-84625-152-8

Published by Day One Publications, Ryelands Road, Leominster, HR6 8NZ
☎ 01568 613 740
FAX 01568 611 473
email—sales@dayone.co.uk
web site—www.dayone.co.uk
North American e-mail—usasales@dayone.co.uk

Cover designed by Wayne McMaster and printed by Gutenberg Press, Malta

COMMENDATION

Stephen McQuoid has tackled an often-neglected yet vitally important issue for the modern church. His approach is, as always, biblically based, yet at the same time he has demonstrated the relevance of the subject through a wide range of illustrations and examples. He emphasizes the need for leaders not to shirk the correction of members, no matter how difficult this may be. In exercising discipline, the church is giving God's verdict on the particular situation. There must, therefore, be both judgement and compassion.

Helpful advice is given to both leaders and members as to what kind of attitude should be displayed towards the offender. This short book is remarkably comprehensive in its treatment of the subject. I have no hesitation in commending it.

David Clarkson, elder at Cartsbridge Evangelical Church, Busby, Glasgow, and author of the Learning to Lead *course.*

In any local church, the issues of authority, discipline and leadership lie close to the surface. Church members and leaders alike seek to act biblically, but relating the various scriptural passages to practical situations poses many challenges. Stephen's book explores succinctly some of the cultural issues, scriptural context and practical outworkings of the vital need to keep the body in shape. I would commend this book wholeheartedly—not only to church leaders who are seeking counsel, but also to church members who are interested in exploring this vital doctrine of the local and universal church.

Andrew Lacey, Church Elder, Manager GLO Book Shop, Director of Partnership, Scotland

Although the examples given in this book are of real situations, all names have been changed to protect the identities of those involved.

CONTENTS

Order in the house of God

If the Church is a living body united to the same head … it is impossible that one part should be independent of all the rest.

–Charles Hodge

I t was every pastor's dream. Mark was a young man who just seemed to love coming to church. What is more, his enthusiasm was contagious. Every time he spoke, it was to say something good about the services or the activities of the church. During one house group, he brought a smile to everyone's face by boldly declaring, 'This is the best church I have ever been to.' But then it all went horribly wrong.

One day, the pastor was teaching about the responsibility that each member of the church carries as a good witness of Jesus Christ. He suggested that, if a church member were to sin openly in some way, the leaders of the church had a duty to deal with the situation and, if necessary, apply discipline. Mark took exception to this. In discussions after the service, he bluntly stated that no one should have the right to tell him what to do with his life and that, if he ever did fall into sin, it was his responsibility to deal with it privately. As far as he was concerned, the only role the church should have would be to encourage members who fell and to pray for their restoration. Any further action would be an intrusion.

Mark no longer attends that church. He is one of a growing number of Christians who so struggle with the issue of church discipline that they have become disillusioned and have left their churches. They are casualties of a contemporary culture that privatizes personal conduct to the point where no one has the right to say anything about anyone, not even in church.

The problem with discipline

This story could be repeated a thousand times over in many

different churches throughout the Western world. Church leaders have frequently had to do battle to maintain the integrity of their churches and, in so doing, they have had to work through the painful process of church discipline, often with tragic results. Experience has taught us that the issue of church discipline is nothing less than tortuous.

So what is it that makes church discipline one of the great difficulties of contemporary church life? Answering this question adequately requires a book in itself, but there are a number of obvious factors that conspire to make church discipline a thorny issue.

PRIDE

First and foremost, there is the issue of pride. The fact is that no one likes to be 'punished' for doing wrong, not least adults. Discipline is a difficult thing to handle and, consequently, when someone is being disciplined by his or her church, that person naturally reacts against the action. This issue is heightened by the fact that most people suffer from a lack of objectivity about their own failings. In most cases, when someone else points out where I have gone wrong, I do not think my faults are as serious as my accuser does. Most people try to justify their own actions, including the ones that are sinful and contrary to biblical teaching. Because they are used to them, they feel comfortable with them. Consequently, they are unable to view them in an objective way.

THE CONTEXT OF SOCIETY

The second thing that makes church discipline difficult is the context of the evil society in which we live. The Bible spares no blushes as it describes human society as utterly fallen and depraved (Rom. 1:18–32). Because we live within society, we are not always aware, even as Christians, of the terrible state society is in. If we could view it through the eyes of Christ, we would quickly realize its fallenness and be appalled. Sadly, however, this clarity of thought is all too uncommon among Christians and, consequently, we perceive things through the lens of contemporary thinking.

It is at this point that we see where the problem lies. Whatever an individual Christian may do in terms of falling, his or her misdemeanour will seem paltry in comparison with the evils of society in general. Any attempts at church discipline will inevitably seem petty and churlish. To use a crude analogy, it is a bit like telling a sewage worker who is wading in some hideous drain that he must floss his teeth because they look unsightly. Church discipline just doesn't seem to make sense, given the moral corruption of our world.

LACK OF OBJECTIVE MORALS

A third and related problem is the lack of objective moral standards within our culture. We no longer live in an age where there is universal agreement about what is right or wrong. Of course, in the past, when such agreement existed, people were no less sinful. But at least they recognized what sin was and that what they were doing was wrong, even though they continued to do it. Today, however, church leaders struggle to convince even church members that sin exists and is offensive to God. Whether it is the sin of gossip, slander, dishonesty, materialism, idolatry, homosexual activity or pre-marital sex, the moral relativity of the age has made any attempt at discipline a thorny issue.

Contemporary biblical scholarship has not always helped. Though I appreciate the learnedness of many of the world's great Bible scholars, it cannot be doubted that scholarship which does not take the Bible seriously has done much to damage the purity of the church. In recent years, a plethora of published works have suggested that we need to add our own input and bias to the biblical text. This is to counter the 'culturally biased perspective' of the biblical writers so that we can find a more 'relevant' interpretation for the present age. For example, some scholars say that Paul came from a background where women were oppressed and so he added this oppression into his writings. We, they say, should therefore note this and remove concepts like 'submission' from our thinking as we apply his writings to today's church. Likewise, they say, Paul came from a context where sexual immorality was shunned (in some circles, at least), and he therefore took a strong line on sex outside marriage and homosexual activity. We, they continue, need to see this context and expunge these prohibitions from any modern reading or application of the text.

Such scholarship is frankly unfaithful to the biblical text. It is entirely wrong arbitrarily to remove truths from the text that we do not like so as to make the Bible more comfortable and accommodating. Biblical interpretation is an important discipline and must be done well. The starting point must be a conviction that the Bible is the infallible and unchanging Word of God and that it must be allowed to say what it says, however unpalatable it might be. If churches do not take the Bible seriously, they will have no objective standard by which they can make judgements about the behaviour of individual members, especially in a culture where no objective moral standards exist.

WESTERN INDIVIDUALISM

A fourth problem we face in relation to discipline is the extreme individualism of Western culture. I have had the privilege of travelling to and working in many different countries. One of the most striking things I have noted is the extent to which many of the cultures I have experienced are corporate in their outlook. For example, I grew up in Ethiopia, where private space is almost non-existent. Everybody is involved in everyone else's business. If you are driving, all your passengers will feel the need to comment on your driving and participate in the experience. If you crash your car in the process, you will immediately be surrounded by a crowd of bystanders, all of them strangers, who will volunteer advice about what to do next, whether that advice was requested or not. Everything is done corporately, for, within that culture, there are no individuals.

In the West, the opposite occurs. We believe in autonomous man. The responsibility for actions rests with the individual. In many ways, this is a very positive thing and can be seen as a strength of Western culture; however, there is a downside. When it comes to the issue of how we relate to one another, words like 'accountability' are unpopular because we want to be accountable only to ourselves. In church life, this poses an obvious problem. When the issue of church discipline arises, people are horrified to discover that they have to answer to others, especially to the leadership of the church. This goes against the grain of everything they feel to be right, and those being disciplined can easily become angered at the unwelcome intrusion of others into their personal affairs.

DEMOCRATIC VIEW OF CHURCH LIFE

This leads us to the fifth problem, which is the way in which our individualistic culture views the role of leadership. As I have already mentioned, I grew up in Ethiopia. For the first eight years of my life, that involved living under the authority of the emperor Haile Selasse. Then the communists took over and I experienced the rather harsher existence of life under a totalitarian Marxist regime. In both cases, authority was not to be questioned. A free press did not exist and orders were neither reinterpreted nor watered down. I now have the privilege of living in the comfortable surroundings of a liberal democracy. Here, the lampooning of politicians and objecting to their policies is part of everyday life. The free press also ravages those in public life of whom it disapproves; consequently, leadership becomes a very tough job indeed. It is not a right, but a dubious privilege.

Churches living in this setting face a significant challenge. Church leaders often struggle to maintain order within their churches because they are not viewed with the respect they deserve. It is not uncommon to find a church where the leadership is often criticized, even publicly, and where the pastor is no more than a moving target. In such contexts, the power lies not with the leaders but with those who want to take potshots at them. The leader must be above reproach, so he is unable to behave in the same way as his opponents; indeed, he is often unable to defend himself. From this vulnerable position, it is very difficult to carry out any effective form of church discipline.

Why should we use discipline in the church?

If one thing is clear so far, it is that church discipline is tough. Maintaining any form of discipline in the church will take both courage and determination. Church leaders will truly have their work cut out for them if they decide that, in some way, church members must be held accountable for their actions. Given this, questions must surely be asked as to why we should bother with church discipline at all.

THE HONOUR OF GOD

The first reason why maintaining church discipline is so important is that we need to have a concern for the honour of God. In 1 Samuel 17, the young shepherd boy David was sent by his father to check on the welfare of his brothers, who were recruits in the Israelite army. As he arrived at the battlefield, he was stunned by what he saw. The Israelites and the Philistines were lined up on either side of the battlefield. The giant Goliath was challenging any individual in the Israelite army to fight him in a representative battle, but none was willing. His huge stature and warlike appearance were more than their courage could confront. Saul had raised the stakes by offering the reward of tax exemption as well as his daughter's hand in marriage, but there were still no takers.

Despite his youth, David was not intimidated by Goliath. But what did concern him was the cowardice of God's people. He described the situation as a 'disgrace': 'What will be done for the man who kills this Philistine and removes this disgrace from Israel? Who is this uncircumcised Philistine that he should defy the armies of the living God?' (v. 26). For David, however, the issue was not that this situation made the men of Israel appear cowardly, but that it reflected badly on God. For Goliath to impose himself as he did was a direct challenge to the 'living God' whose armies he threatened. David was concerned for God's honour, which was being compromised by the behaviour of his people.

This concept can also be seen in the New Testament, where Paul urges believers to 'conduct yourselves in a manner worthy of the gospel of Christ' (Phil. 1:27). The sacrifice of Christ compels us to live in such a way as to demonstrate the power and glory of the gospel. Ultimately, our lives will have a bearing on the credibility of the Christian faith. As Jesus said in Matthew 5:16, 'let your light shine before men, that they may see your good deeds and praise your Father in heaven'; we are to live in such a way that people recognize God's hand in our lives and praise him for what he is doing in us.

Our concern for God's honour should be the primary motivation for having a disciplined church. The church belongs to God, not to any individual or group of individuals. We are the bride of Christ (2 Cor. 11:2; Rev. 19:7; 21:2), and when we live lives that are unholy and inappropriate, we dishonour God. The church is a billboard declaring the glory of God. If the message being communicated does not reflect something of the glory and majesty of God, his honour is at stake.

THE REPUTATION OF THE CHURCH

Closely linked to the honour of God is the reputation of the actual church. The church needs to have credibility for its own sake. If it has no credibility, it will not be an attractive witness to a needy world. No one will be persuaded by the church's proclamation of the gospel if those who comprise its membership do not demonstrate the power of the gospel in their own lives. The church is also a voice in society, providing a conscience and correcting injustice. But if the church loses its moral authority because of the behaviour of some of its members, its voice will be muffled and its impact minimized.

I recently attended a conference in one of the oldest and most Catholic cities in North America. As I walked around the city, I was impressed by the sheer number of Catholic churches, monasteries, convents, schools, colleges and even a Catholic university. I said to my guide, 'The Catholic church must be one of the must potent forces for good in the city.' She responded rather melancholically by saying that the impact of the church had been greatly reduced in recent years because of allegations of priests involved in child abuse. These were not dealt with properly and consequently the church lost any credibility in the eyes of the community. A church with no credibility cannot function properly; its potential and attractiveness are simply lost.

THE HEALTH OF THE BODY

Another reason for good discipline in the church is the health of the body. One of the most powerful images in the New Testament is that of the church as a body (1 Cor. 12). We are not just a collection of individuals thrown together for some kind of religious experience; rather, we are an organic unity. Through the blood of Christ and the unifying power of the Holy Spirit we find oneness. We are able to feed off one another, to benefit from the mutual encouragement that being together brings.

Of course, the opposite is also true. Although we can have

a beneficial effect on one another, if one member of the body is spiritually sick, he or she can also cause great damage to the rest of the body. In 1 Corinthians 12:26 Paul says, 'If one part suffers, every part suffers with it.' This can be applied in a number of ways. Certainly, there should be such a quality of relationships within the church that, if one member is suffering in some way, the other members should have such empathy that they feel the pain of their fellow brother or sister. But, equally, we are so closely knit together that we actually have an impact on one another, whether for good or ill. For the sake of the wider church, therefore, discipline must at times be applied so that the 'body life' of the church remains healthy.

In a church near where I live, the elders had to ban a young woman from the services because her actions and influence were so pernicious that she was having a hugely detrimental impact on all with whom she came into contact. Though rare, sometimes such strong measures are required to keep the body healthy.

THE UNITY OF THE SPIRIT

Another reason that necessitates the application of discipline is the unity of the Spirit. Paul is clear in Ephesians that we are joined by the Spirit, who makes us one: 'Make every effort to keep the unity of the Spirit through the bond of peace. There is one body and one Spirit—just as you were called to one hope when you were called—one Lord, one faith, one baptism' (Eph. 4:3–5). In any family, however, there can be issues that bring stress to relationships. In my experience, few things cause more disunity than when one member of the church is living a lifestyle that is obviously wrong. The divisiveness comes from various angles. To begin with, the individual concerned will be spiritually hampered by the sin and will therefore not be enjoying a close walk with Jesus Christ. This makes that person less able to engage meaningfully and lovingly with fellow Christians. Secondly, that person's lifestyle will inevitably

15

lead to gossip within the church which is, by its very nature, destructive. Thirdly, once the devil gets a foothold in the door of the church, he will exploit this gap to the maximum by doing as much damage to the individual and the church as possible. He will drive a wedge between the fallen church member and the rest of the body, thus causing feelings of isolation and rejection. Clearly, any sense of unity which the church members feel will be under threat if the situation continues.

THE SPIRITUAL LIFE OF THE INDIVIDUAL

While thinking of the damage that can be caused to a church if discipline is not applied, we also need to think about the damage that is done to the individual. At the heart of any sinful situation is an individual who is struggling in his or her walk with Christ. Those of us who are parents can understand the situation well. When our children do wrong, we recognize the need to discipline them. We do not punish them to cause harm; rather, it is because we love them and we want the best for them. We want them to live fruitful and successful lives. Likewise, we need to apply discipline in the life of the church because the sin of any individual affects that individual first of all. The application of discipline is to enable him or her to come back to a close relationship with Christ and to continue in the Christian life. It is, therefore, a real act of love.

THE WITNESS TO THE SPIRITUAL REALM

A final reason for applying discipline in the life of the church is because of the great crowd of witnesses who watch the church live out its existence. It is difficult to read the New Testament without becoming aware of the presence in the world of spiritual forces both good and bad (Eph. 6:12). We do not exist within a purely physical realm; angels and demons, messengers of God and demonic powers inhabit our realm and interact with us. There are also many hints in the Bible that these spiritual forces are keen observers of human life. They see what we do and react to it (Job 1:9–11; 1 Peter 1:12).

These spiritual forces are alert to the failings of Christians. The demons tempt Christians to sin and gloat when they fall. The angels, on the other hand, are sent to protect believers and rejoice when they experience personal victories in their lives. In each case, these opposing powers have a vested interest in what goes on. It is at this point that church discipline becomes important. When churches become complacent about sin, the forces of hell celebrate; but when churches take seriously their responsibility to live for Christ, the angels rejoice and heaven rings with the glory of God. The spirit forces are therefore also affected by the use or absence of church discipline.

A new conceptual framework for discipline

Having stated the importance of church discipline, we need to recognize that, given our present culture, discipline will be a difficult thing to maintain. Perhaps one way forward is to understand where the church fits into culture and then find ways of marrying the demands of the Bible with the reality of culture.

Firstly, then, we need to reflect on the role of the church within a culture. In doing so, we must recognize that there are two extremes that we need to avoid. The first is that of *cultural submersion*. By this we mean that a church could be so slavishly trying to adhere to its culture that it allows the demands of culture to dictate how the church should operate. A church might do this for perfectly good motives. For example, the members of a church could be so motivated to reach people within their community that they strive for ever-greater relevance, going the extra mile to make the church attractive. This desire is certainly good. However, we should question whether a church should model itself on the prevailing culture rather than on the Bible. Jesus was radical precisely because he was not a slave to culture. There is a real sense in which the church should be countercultural and therefore not just submerge itself culturally.

The second extreme could be termed *cultural aversion*. By this we mean that a church could be so distinct and different as to be utterly irrelevant to society. Again, this problem can occur out of a pure motive. The Bible tells us that we are not to 'love the world' (1 John 2:15). A church may be so determined not to love the world that it utterly rejects anything that is not overtly Christian. In their appropriate enthusiasm for holiness, however, the members develop a myriad of rules that enable them, as far as they can judge, to live a life so stringent that they are simply not able to be anything other than holy. The trouble is that the Bible has fewer rules than they imagine and it does not cover every contingency in a neatly packaged way. Their rule book must therefore, of necessity, be man-made rather than divinely inspired. This has the effect of isolating them from society at large as well as from anyone who does not match up to their rather artificial standards. A church like this might, in theory, be disciplined, but it will not have an environment where genuine spiritual development can take place.

The middle road between these extremes is *countercultural integration*. This is when a church sees the Bible, and not culture, as the source of authority, yet recognizes that spirituality needs to be incarnated within a cultural setting so that church practice takes account of culture. This balance is, of course, difficult to maintain, and in reality churches learn to operate like this on a trial-and-error basis. It is not a neatly packaged way of doing church. However, it is a model that is biblically faithful and at the same time allows for the fact that we live in an imperfect, fallen world.

If this is the model we wish to follow, when it comes to the issue of church discipline we need to learn to use language and modes of expression that can be culturally understood and appreciated. We need to picture church discipline in positive as well as negative terms. Both are important and biblical, and the barriers that have already been identified will be weakened if the picture we paint of discipline is one that does not just contain censure. Two contemporary pictures that can be readily identified with and appreciated within our culture are those of a *disciplined athlete* and a *life coach*.

Athlete

Few in our sports-mad society will not be able to identify, in some small way at least, with an athlete or sportsman or woman. It is hard to watch television or listen to the radio without hearing some mention of football, athletics, boxing, rugby or other sport. The athletes involved in sport are 'A-list' celebrities and are greatly admired. No one would be naive enough to suppose that these athletes achieved what they did by being couch potatoes! On the contrary, in their quest for excellence they have made great sacrifices, worked hard and led highly disciplined lives so that they could achieve their goals. However we might complain about the money sports stars earn, no one can fail to admire their commitment.

The issue of discipline can fruitfully be conveyed in these terms. Discipline is not just about 'telling people off' for their bad behaviour; rather, we want people to excel, to drive themselves towards excellence. The church should motivate people to live in such a way that they are heading towards the finishing line and the prize that lies ahead (Phil. 3:12–14). We can harness the individualism of our culture as we encourage people to take responsibility for their actions.

Life coach

A second picture that we can emphasize is that of a life coach. People within our society are increasingly looking for meaning and purpose in their lives. They want to rise above the mundane and live lives that count for something. Life coaches exist for just this purpose. One life-coaching website I found stated that 'life coaching aims to help you achieve clarity and confidence to work through issues that are holding you back from enjoying a challenging and harmonious life'. I can think of few better ways of describing what church discipline is all about.

Church discipline does not exist so that leaders of churches can frustrate their members or make them feel totally inadequate. Rather, church leaders should picture themselves as life coaches enabling church members to see clearly the most exciting and fulfilling way of living, which involves living according to God's master plan. Discipline will involve working through issues that are holding Christians back from enjoying a challenging and harmonious Christian life. We can harness the desire for fulfilment and purpose which is very real within our society to enable people within the church to live dynamic and vibrant lives.

These two pictures enable us to communicate the issue of church discipline in a positive and culturally relevant way, while at the same time conveying biblical truth. Paul himself used the analogy of an athlete as he talked about Christian living (Phil. 3:12–14; 2 Tim. 2:5). Likewise, Jesus stated that the best way to save our lives is to lose them (Mark 8:35; Matt. 16:24–26), thus challenging us to find real life as a daily reality. If we communicate the positives of church discipline, it will help us to make it a reality in the life of our churches.

A biblical theology of correction

This Bible is for the government of the people, by the people and for the people.

–John Wycliffe

A ny attempt to look at the issue of church discipline must inevitably begin with Scripture. It is there that we find the template by which we operate. The theology of church discipline is rooted in the wider biblical theme of God who has a right to expect obedience and will act when it is not forthcoming. In order to tease out this bigger picture, we need to begin, not in the New Testament, but in the Old. Our starting point is not with God's dealing with Israel, but with his dealings with man in general. This is because God is not merely holy, he is also the Lord of all; we need to think about the implications of this in general before focusing specifically on God's relationship with his chosen people.

God and the Old Testament people of God

GOD AS CREATOR

We turn, therefore, to the account of the Fall, which demonstrates both the need for and the nature of God's discipline. The creation narrative clearly demonstrates what we know from personal experience, that when God created human beings, he gave them free will. This freedom meant that the range of choices which humans had at their disposal included the choice to reject God and to be disobedient to his will. This was the path the human race chose through our first parents, Adam and Eve, and the inevitable Fall brought with it the disastrous consequences of alienation from God and death. It must be stated that, in the creation account, sin was not just something that offended God, but also something that deprived people of the very best—a living relationship with him.

The account, however, did not end with the Fall; rather, this was only the opening scene. Just when all seemed to be lost, we find God looking for Adam (Gen. 3:9). God pronounced sentence on Adam and Eve because of their sin (3:16–19), but also provided clothes for them made from animal skin. These were primarily coverings to hide the shame of their nakedness but, as the garments were made from animal skin, here was an early indication that the death of one creature was needed to cover the shame of another.[1]

Here is the establishing of a pattern that will repeat itself throughout Scripture: as people fall and sin, so God deals with that sin in judgement. But judgement need not be the final action; indeed, God does not want the story to finish with judgement. Within God's grace, there is the desire for renewal and restoration.

GOD AS REDEEMER

Genesis 6 is the next occasion on which we see this cycle occurring. The degeneration of the human race could be seen in the perversity of this ancient society (vv. 5–6). God decided to act in judgement by sending a severe flood which would wipe out the inhabitants of the earth. There was one man who did please God: Noah, a righteous man who had resisted the allure of his corrupt society. In response to Noah's blameless life, God provided salvation in the midst of the judgement that was to come.

This salvation would come in the form of an ark which Noah was commanded to build. The presence of the ark did not remove the need for judgement; rather, it demonstrated that, even in the midst of judgement and its aftermath, there was hope. Noah and his family took refuge in the ark during the flood and, when they came through unscathed, they offered up a sacrifice of thanks to God for the salvation he had provided.[2] Just as God had envisioned what would be after the judgement that befell

Adam and Eve, so he took Noah and his family through this judgement to a place where they could thrive once more.

GOD AS SANCTIFIER

Both of these accounts demonstrate God's dealing with mankind as a whole. As the biblical narrative unfolded, however, God narrowed his focus and chose a people who would be his in a special way. This was done by establishing a covenant with Abraham. This was not an exclusive relationship, for in choosing Abraham and his descendents, God's purpose was that all nations would be blessed (Gen. 12:3). The significance of this point must be recognized because, not only do we see the same pattern of fall, judgement and restoration being played out in the history of the nation of Israel, but we also see a nation that was a role model, revealing something of God's character and purposes to the wider world. This was a mantle which would ultimately be taken on by the New Testament church. Like Israel, the church exists to be a light to the nations, and it is through the church that God reveals his glory to the world and draws people into a relationship with him (2 Cor. 5:20). The church also needs to remain holy because this is her calling (1 Peter 2:5). If this does not happen, God must act, as the church, like Israel before her, is part of God's plan for world redemption.

Once again, the pattern that began in the early chapters of Genesis is repeated throughout the history of Israel. From the time of Exodus 20 onwards, when Moses delivered the law, no one within that nation could have had any doubts concerning what God expected of them. It was also made clear that their success would be determined by the extent to which they complied with the law. If they were obedient, they could expect God's protection and blessing; but if they were disobedient, God would deal with them.

Rather predictably, they fell and God had to respond. The

Old Testament prophets were sent to declare the imminence of God's judgement. They took the role of prosecution lawyers, laying out the case before the nation and passing sentence. Ultimately, sentence came in the form of the exile. The land which the nation possessed, and which was the embodiment of God's blessings, was taken from them and they ended up in a foreign land.

The pattern continued here, too. Many of the prophets finished their pronouncements on a high note, assuring the people that, in days to come, there would yet be blessings (see Amos 9:11–15). God had not abandoned them; rather, they would experience his blessings again once they recognized their mistakes and repented. Here, on a national scale, the fall, judgement and restoration pattern was played out.

Approaching the New Testament church

Given the pattern which is so clearly demonstrated in the Old Testament, it is unsurprising that the New Testament continues this theme within the context of church life. God requires of churches that they live holy lives and demands that appropriate action be taken when they fail to do so (1 Cor. 1:2 ; Rev. 3:19). He is being entirely consistent with his actions throughout biblical history beginning with the Fall. Every case of church discipline must be seen in this regard. If we as a church feel the need to deal with someone in the church because he or she has fallen, we are not simply punishing that person in isolation; rather, we are reflecting the way in which a holy God relates to his fallen creatures. Church discipline, therefore, is an outcome of applied theology; it is God's nature incarnated within a local-church setting.

Biblical pictures of discipline

SHEPHERDS OF THE FLOCK

Having noted the biblical theme of fall, judgement and

restoration, we now reflect on some other themes which relate to the issue of discipline. The first of these is that of a shepherd. Throughout Scripture, we frequently encounter shepherds because much of the Bible is set within an agricultural society. However, the job of a shepherd is metaphorically applied to God. Most notably in Psalm 23, the shepherd is pictured as carefully and lovingly tending the sheep, a metaphorical term for the people of God.

In the New Testament, the metaphor of a shepherd is applied specifically to Christ, who is the great Shepherd of the sheep (Heb. 13:20). Much could be said about the shepherd's role but, at the heart of it, a shepherd has to guide the sheep into situations where they can feed safely, and enable them to avoid danger.

In the specific context of the local church, leaders are referred to as shepherds of God's flock ('Be shepherds of God's flock', 1 Peter 5:2). They have the responsibility under Christ to ensure the spiritual safety of God's people. This image does not fit comfortably with our individualistic culture, where everyone wants to act autonomously; however, one reason for using sheep as a metaphor for believers is that sheep, if left unchecked, will wander off and get themselves into difficulties. Anyone who has been a church leader or pastor for any length of time will understand this point well. It is the job of a shepherd to provide positive direction in the lives of the flock, even if that input is not always appreciated. This will, at times, result in the application of church discipline. Given the shepherd motif, the work of church leaders should be seen against the backdrop of God's governance of his people.

It must be emphasized, however, that pastors and church leaders need to be people of quality if their discipline is to be effective. Throughout the Old Testament, there are examples of spiritual leaders who were not men of God. In 1 Samuel 2:12–17, for example, Eli's sons carried no moral authority because of their lifestyles. When we come to the New Testament, we find

Paul urging Timothy to become a worker approved by God so that he can carry out his ministry with integrity: 'Do your best to present yourself to God as one approved, a workman who does not need to be ashamed and who correctly handles the word of truth' (2 Tim. 2:15).

Sadly, I have encountered situations where church leaders have carried out discipline yet, in doing so, they have shown themselves to be hypocritical, for their own lives have been far from what God expects. Not that leaders must be perfect— clearly, that is impossible—but they must be good examples, otherwise it will be a case of the blind leading the blind. Their role in carrying out church discipline must be fulfilled with humility and compassion for, as Jesus himself said, 'in the same way you judge others, you will be judged, and with the measure you use, it will be measured to you' (Matt. 7:2).

Moreover, we should not forget that the moral authority which a church leader carries comes not from his office but from a Christlike life. Only then can he inspire those he cares for to achieve excellence for God. One man I know achieves this balance very well. He is the leader of a small church in the middle of a sprawling housing estate replete with social problems. Most members of the congregation are young and are the only Christians in their families. Given their lack of spiritual support at home, Jim is diligent at keeping in touch with them. He also tells them very openly what kind of lifestyle God expects from them. The great thing is that Jim himself is a man of great integrity, so much so that even the non-Christians who attend church express their admiration of him. If someone does fall in some way, Jim is quick to visit that person, not to condemn but to help that person get back on his or her feet spiritually. This is not a compromise; rather, it focuses on the goal of restoration. Whatever measures Jim feels are necessary as far as discipline is concerned, he never takes his eyes off the restoration goal.

PRIESTHOOD OF ALL BELIEVERS

Another theme which winds its way through the Bible's narrative is that of priesthood. Once the children of Israel were established as the people of God, they began to set up a priesthood which would conduct and order the religious life of the community (Exod. 28:1). This was not without antecedents, for as far back as Genesis, Abraham benefited from the priestly function of Melchizedek (Gen. 14:18–20). The priests had the function of representing the people before God and dealing with the issue of the people's sin. They offered sacrifices on behalf of penitents and presented their cases before God. In this way, priests involved themselves in the lives of people when sin was an issue.

When we come to the New Testament, the idea of priesthood continued, even though the old religious system with its rituals was done away with (Heb. 8:13). Here two new ideas are introduced. Firstly, Jesus himself is the great high priest who offers up himself as a sacrifice for our sin: 'Day after day every priest stands and performs his religious duties; again and again he offers the same sacrifices, which can never take away sins. But when this priest had offered for all time one sacrifice for sins, he sat down at the right hand of God' (Heb. 10:11–12). Secondly, the priesthood was extended to incorporate all believers: 'But you are a chosen people, a royal priesthood, a holy nation, a people belonging to God, that you may declare the praises of him who called you out of darkness into his wonderful light' (1 Peter 2:9). Every believer has the job of ministering to other Christians, representing them before God, encouraging them in holiness and helping them to deal with the great problem of sin in their lives. It is therefore appropriate for every member of a church to play some part in encouraging fellow Christians when they fall. Though the shepherds/elders have the primary responsibility and are guardians of the church's reputation, the role is one that we all share; when we do so, we continue the work of the priesthood which God himself established early in the Old Testament.

This, of course, requires a significant change of perspective in most churches. I remember many occasions when I was an elder and someone in the church would say to me, 'This person needs a visit' or 'I am a little worried about her and I think you should speak to her and tell her not to do it.' I was glad that concern was being demonstrated and, of course, as an elder, I was delighted to be able to help where appropriate. More often than not, however, I would ask the person, 'Why haven't you gone to visit that person? After all, you are a priest.' It is at such moments that we realize that, although we talk about the priesthood of all believers, often we don't really believe in it. It is a biblical concept, however, so we should believe in it and should all be active in caring for one another as priests. As Martin Luther once said, 'Even a shoemaker can be a priest of God.'

Preventive discipline

Chapter 3

Innocence is like polished armour; it adorns and defends.

–Bishop Robert South

Many years ago, I used to work as a nurse for the NHS. Since those days, many things have changed in health care, some good and some not so good. One of the good changes has been a renewed emphasis on preventive health care: resources are put into programmes which prevent people from getting sick as well as ones that make them better. This, it seems to me, is a good thing. If we can strive to keep people healthy, we will have to pay less in hospital bills and needless suffering will be prevented. Living as I do in the outskirts of Glasgow, where heart disease is rife and lung cancer is a big issue, I am all in favour of promoting preventive health care. Whether it is the adverts that tell us to 'choose the school walk rather than the school run', or courses that enable smokers to stop and overweight people to lose a few pounds, it is all for the benefit of the nation's health.

When it comes to the spiritual health of the church, the same principle applies. It is not sufficient to discipline people only once they have fallen; we must also try to prevent sin from creeping into the church in the first place. Prevention is always better than cure, and this prevention should be seen as a form of discipline. In essence, discipline is not just about punishing, but rather it is a whole way of life which keeps us spiritually accountable and in a right relationship with God. If we are vigilant in our preventive discipline, we will have fewer crisis points when someone in the church begins to sin and then requires corrective discipline. What will preventive discipline involve?

Teaching

The first element that we need to focus on is teaching. Unless people within our churches know what God expects of them, they will not be in a position to live it out. Interestingly, in the Great Commission of Matthew 28:18–20, Jesus specified that his disciples were to go into all the world *teaching*, so that his followers would be well aware of their responsibilities. It is said that knowledge is power; certainly in the Christian life, to know how we should live is to have a focus which leads to correct living.

If the teaching programme in a church is so important, it stands to reason that it should be well thought out and not arbitrary. In education, a great deal of time is spent thinking about how students should be taught and what the curriculum should contain. Each subject is carefully chosen, each course has a rationale behind it, each class has a teaching plan complete with educational outcomes and assessments. If we truly think that our spiritual health is of equal importance to the physical lives we live, then the same care and attention should go into planning the teaching programme of a local church. As Summerton comments, 'The boredom and impatience of many ordinary church members with the teaching which they receive can often be traced to the shortcomings of those who teach, to the imperfect understanding of the teachers of their responsibilities, and to their penchant for making dull what should be lively, exciting and vibrant.'[3]

The importance of a well-thought-out teaching programme was impressed upon me recently when invited to preach at a nearby church. Because I knew the elders well, a couple of them shared some of their concerns with me for my prayers. One of the most difficult situations they were trying to deal with was one in which a man who had been twice divorced was wanting to remarry. This was giving them much food for thought as they were trying to work out what to do in the situation. Out of interest, I asked them when they last had teaching in the church on the issue of marriage, divorce and remarriage. I was startled to discover that none of them could remember. This was an important lesson. I am not suggesting that, had they done some teaching on the issue, this situation would not have presented itself; they would probably, however, have been better prepared for it.

There are a number of things that we need to think about in this regard. Firstly, there is the issue of how to teach. Many churches put a great deal of emphasis on preaching as a medium for communication. This is good because it is both a biblical and effective way of communicating Christian truth. Good preaching also has unparalleled motivational power. Preaching on its own, however, is not sufficient to meet the demands of contemporary church life. The preaching programme needs to be supplemented with other methods such as small Bible study groups, mentor groups and one-to-one discipleship, so that what is taught can then be applied to everyday life.

Secondly, there is the issue of what to teach. In the life of the church, the whole Bible needs to be covered, as all Scripture is inspired and is profitable (2 Tim. 3:16). We do, however, need to think about the emphasis we give to different sections of Scripture. For example, we will not treat the book of Philippians in the same way in which we treat the book of Leviticus. Different Bible books or passages will achieve different purposes in the lives of members of the congregation. We also need to bring different emphases out of the passages we teach, so that Scripture is applied practically to people's lives. I generally find it helpful to have the following categories in the back of my mind as I think about the church's teaching programme:

BIBLICAL-FOUNDATIONAL

The first category I call 'biblical-foundational' because these passages or books contain material that generally builds up the knowledge of people within the church. These passages might include material that deals with who God is, who we are, the creation, Old Testament history, New Testament history, the time of the Old Testament prophets and legal/cultic passages such as the book of Leviticus. In other words, these are Bible passages and sections of Scripture that give people a general knowledge of the Bible's storyline and setting. The lessons should be applied to our lives, but the actual body of information is vital for a healthy Christian life.

SPIRITUALLY ENHANCING

Secondly, there is the category that I call 'spiritually enhancing' material. Of course, all of Scripture is spiritually enhancing, but there are some passages which, when communicated, have a particular impact on our Christian lives. I recently heard a series of sermons on the book of Isaiah. The preacher was using the book as a platform to express something of the greatness and faithfulness of God. Even as he spoke, I felt that my heart was being lifted. The praise sessions which came before and after the preaching were electric. We were all so spiritually uplifted by the impact of the Word of God on our lives that we could not help but praise God. Such teaching which focuses on the greatness of God and our response to him will keep us walking closely with Christ and away from sin.

ETHICAL

Thirdly, there is ethical teaching. This is totally different from the previous two categories. It neither excites us nor simply lays a foundation of knowledge. Rather, it tells us about how we should be living our lives on a daily basis. There are many Bible passages and even whole books that deal with subjects such as divorce, homosexuality, stealing, dishonesty, slander and issues relating to social justice. These, though unpleasant topics, need to be part of a church's teaching programme. Once people within the church understand what is expected of them, there is a simple choice to make: either they choose to obey God, or they choose to disobey. Whichever decision is made, it will not be uninformed.

CAUTIONARY

Finally, there is cautionary teaching. This category is important, not least because it is so prevalent in the Bible. It is wonderful to read passages about God's love, grace and kindness. At the same time, however, we need to take seriously those many passages that warn us that there are serious consequences when we allow sin into our lives. Ultimately, these passages are meant for our own good. Just as a parent might say to a child, 'Don't do that, or else ...', so these cautionary passages warn us of the consequences of allowing sin to come into our lives. Cautionary passages make it clear that all of our actions have consequences and that disobedience to God can bring about spiritual disaster. To be forewarned is to be forearmed. It is, therefore, a healthy part of a church's diet to be warned against living in a way that displeases God.

If we teach through the Bible systematically, all these issues will be dealt with sooner or later. The danger of being too subject-oriented is that we are always looking for catchy titles to sermons in order to make them sound attractive. Then we run the risk of missing important sections of Scripture. We need to remember that all Scripture is God-breathed and profitable (2 Tim. 3:16). There is, however, a need for balance. We should commit ourselves to teaching the whole Bible, but at the same time remain aware of what the church needs at any given time. We should ensure that each of the four categories mentioned above gets an appropriate hearing throughout the year. This balance will be one of the best protections against sin creeping into the church.

Pastoral care

Having considered the role that teaching plays in disciplining the church, we now move onto the area of pastoral care. It is interesting to note that the apostles in general, and Paul in particular, spent time going from house to house, encouraging and instructing Christians: 'Day after day, in the temple courts and from house to house, they never stopped teaching and proclaiming the good news that Jesus is the Christ' (Acts 5:42); 'You know that I have not hesitated to preach anything that would be helpful to you but have taught you publicly and from house to house' (20:20). This is of vital importance because experience suggests that church life is all about relationships. It is as the pastor or leaders of a church relate to the members that they are able to build them up and encourage them to live for Christ. There is also a direct link between pastoral care and the relevance of a teaching programme. As I spend time with members of my church, I get an idea of the kinds of things that are troubling them. I am then able to apply Scripture in a more focused way in my preaching. The most powerful preachers, therefore, are not the greatest orators, but the ones who combine their preaching ministry with a practical pastoral concern for their congregations. This pastoral care must also stem from a genuine love for those who are being cared for. As Oden comments, 'Neither analytical skill nor theoretical knowledge can have positive effect if there is no genuine love and compassionate care for others.'[4]

When it comes to using pastoral care as a form of preventive discipline, there are three principles that need to be applied. Firstly, there is the principle of knowledge. It is important to know your congregation. It goes without saying that, if church leaders have no idea who they are dealing with, they will be of little practical help. We need to know the strengths and weaknesses of our church members and the spiritual resources they have that will enable them to live successfully for Christ. A basic knowledge of the kinds of people with which we are entrusted will enable us to act in an appropriate way towards them.

A second principle that we need to apply is that of anticipation. We need to be able to think ahead and anticipate specific problems which may arise. This is more than just knowing about a person; rather, it is about seeing potential obstacles or pitfalls which may potentially derail that person in his or her spiritual walk. This takes a great deal of pastoral sensitivity. Just because someone has a weakness in a particular area, it does not necessarily follow that he or she will inevitably fall.

I have a Christian friend who is an alcoholic. Clearly, alcohol has been a danger area in her life in the past. However, she realizes the problem and is very disciplined with herself. In twenty-five years of being a Christian, she has never once touched a drop of alcohol. Anyone who knows her will realize that the issue of alcohol, though a serious and chronic one, will not necessarily be the problem area in her spiritual walk. There will be other issues for her, and those who pastor her need to have enough sensitivity to her life to be able to identify ahead of time what kinds of personal crises she will face.

A third principle is the 'nip-it-in-the-bud' principle. This involves dealing with an issue before it becomes a pastoral crisis. I have witnessed many situations in church life where alarm bells were ringing about someone yet nothing was done and so the situation was allowed to escalate. By the time action was taken, it was too late for preventive discipline; a much more strident approach was necessary.

In one such situation, a young couple at Bible college were preparing to go out to the mission field. They planned to marry at the end of their studies and then go abroad to serve God. It was noticed by both their church leaders and the Bible college staff that they were spending a lot of time alone together, often late at night in their apartments. Nothing was said, not least because no one believed that such a committed young couple was capable of sinning sexually. Suddenly, in their final year, news broke that the girl had become pregnant. They never did make it to the mission field, and, in truth, the fault was not all theirs. Issues must be nipped in the bud by loving pastoral carers before they escalate into crises.

Discipleship

Related to the issue of pastoral care is the more specific role of discipleship. When all is said and done, the most important resource we have in keeping us from falling is a vibrant Christian life. Discipleship therefore needs to be a priority in the life of a church. There are many myths that surround the issue of spiritual growth; one is that spiritual growth will happen automatically so long as someone is faithfully attending church. This is simply not the case. Spiritual maturity develops when someone purposefully commits him- or herself to achieving it. This is what Paul meant when he urged the Philippians, 'Therefore, my dear friends, as you have always obeyed … continue to work out your salvation with fear and trembling' (Phil. 2:12). Not that we work for salvation, but that we, as saved people, work at the implications of being followers of Jesus Christ. It is the balance between a focused spiritual life and the dynamic of the Holy Spirit that changes us and makes us like Christ. Inevitably, this involves discipleship.

Discipleship is not just for new Christians but for the whole church. We all need to grow more; indeed, it is entirely possible for Christians to regress spiritually. There is no direct correlation between the length of time a person has been a Christian and the level of his or her spiritual maturity. People who have been Christians for many years can still be spiritually immature. What is needed is a quality of Christian experience and this, over a sustained period, produces spiritual maturity.

In turn, spiritual maturity enables Christians to withstand temptation and live holy lives. Of course, this is not a given; we are all capable of falling, however strong our spiritual lives are. But a church filled with spiritually mature people will be in much better health and be much less likely to need discipline than one that is not. It is, therefore, a dereliction of duty for a church leader, or group of leaders, not to work hard at discipleship.

Maintaining an effective programme of discipleship in a local church takes a lot of time and energy. It is more than merely expecting people to attend meetings. When Jesus called the Twelve to be his disciples, he poured his life into them. They were taught by him, but they also saw him living out his life in close proximity to them. He was a role model of godliness and they learned as much from his example as from his words. He saw them as friends and had a quality of relationship with them that enabled him to inspire them in their walk with God. However we organize our discipleship programmes, these elements need to be present. In my own church, each member is linked to another in a mutual mentoring relationship. This enables them to feel a sense of spiritual accountability to each other which, in turn, leads to a deeper commitment to Christ. However it is implemented, a good discipleship model will pay dividends.

Community life

Another aspect of preventive discipline is that which is played by the community at large. We have already noted that the New Testament clearly teaches the priesthood of all believers. All of us as Christians are responsible for one another. We all have a role to play encouraging one another to excel in our spiritual lives. The church is also a body that works in unison in order to serve God:

> The body is a unit, though it is made up of many parts; and though all its parts are many, they form one body ... God has combined the members of the body ... so that there should be no division in the body, but that its parts should have equal concern for each other. If one part suffers, every part suffers with it; if one part is honoured, every part rejoices with it. Now you are the body of Christ, and each one of you is a part of it.
>
> 1 Cor. 12:12, 24–27

Communities do not just happen automatically; they only come together through the process of shared experience. This becomes obvious when visiting the many shiny new housing developments in the leafy suburbs of some large cities, where neighbours are strangers to one another and feel no sense of community. Likewise, in the church, a sense of community does not come about automatically. Even though church members share a common commitment to Jesus Christ and a desire to serve him, the fact that they are so different and live such separate lives means that they will not get to know one another just because they are in the same church. I have visited many churches where the members know almost nothing about one another and spend no quality time together.

Where there is no real sense of community in a church, the possibility of members helping one another to live successful Christian lives is greatly reduced. This is an issue that must be dealt with for the sake of the church's spiritual health, though it will not happen swiftly. People are human and not robotic; relationships require time and effort to develop, and no timescale can be put on this process. It can still, however, be a deliberate process in which the church attempts to achieve certain goals. Three in particular are worth considering:

Firstly, it is important to create a sense of accountability within the church. In the account of Cain and Abel, one brother kills the other out of jealousy and is confronted by God, who asks about the brother. In reply, Cain asks, 'Am I my brother's keeper?' (Gen. 4:9). Such distance had crept between them that Cain felt no sense of responsibility towards his brother. This kind of attitude exists within churches and is a significant barrier to any form of community discipline. A sense of accountability must be built into the collective psyche of the church.

Accountability is a two-way process and both streams must be encouraged. Each member must feel a sense of accountability to speak out when something is not right and to challenge when seeing a fellow church member doing something that is not spiritually helpful. Likewise, each member should feel a sense of accountability or duty to the church as a whole to live a holy life, one that does not reflect badly on the church's reputation. Once both of these are in place, the church is in a position to deal with issues before they become crises.

Secondly, this sense of accountability must be tempered by love and trust if it is to work properly. A friend of mine was spoken to by a fellow Christian because something that he was doing was not right. He was neither embarrassed nor angered by the rebuke, as he felt genuinely cared for by the Christian who did the correcting and had enough confidence in him to cope with the vulnerability of correction. Indeed, the incident brought them even closer together and enhanced their relationship because the two of them realized just how much they meant to each other. An atmosphere of love and trust will ensure that Christians will correct but will not become judgemental.

Thirdly, empathy needs to be cultivated. Even where love exists, there can be impatience. This adds strain to the relationship and can cause the people involved eventually to become embittered. However, if there is empathy, if the person doing the correcting can try to understand the weakness and struggle of the Christian who has fallen, then his or her reproach will be gentle and compassionate. If this is also done with a forgiving spirit, the two people will not be distanced from each other as a result of what happens.

These attitudes and qualities need to be sewn into the life of the church at all times. Their value becomes apparent when someone steps out of line and needs to be helped back into a right relationship with God, but the work of installing them requires continual attention. If a church is always working on its internal relationships and ensuring that its members relate to one another in appropriate ways, then, when a crisis does come, that church will be well equipped to deal with it.

Corrective discipline

Chapter 4

A coach is someone who can give correction without causing resentment.

–John Wooden

The very first ward on which I worked when I began my nursing career was one which specialized in dealing with cancer patients. I have to confess that the very thought of working there filled me with a sense of dread. There can be few more emotive words than 'cancer'. It has an impact on people like almost no other. Of course, many people who suffer from this disease can be treated and recover fully. However, it can also be such a serious illness that the staff on my ward had to be very careful about how we communicated information to the patients and their relatives, lest we caused them unnecessary stress.

For many of our patients, their prognosis necessitated surgery. This, of course, is a radical form of treatment which should not be taken lightly because, by its very nature, it is invasive. What I found interesting, however, was that few patients were reticent or scared of surgery in this situation, such was the comparative fear with which they regarded their cancer. One patient in particular comes to mind. He was an elderly gentleman who had never spent a day in hospital in his life. As a result of some tests, it was discovered that he had prostate cancer. When the surgeon informed him that he would have to undergo an operation, the man was greatly relieved. 'That's OK,' he said, 'at least I can definitely be rid of it.' His perspective was a sensible one. No one likes coming under the knife on an operating table, but if someone is suffering from a dangerous condition that can be cured through surgery, it unquestionably becomes the lesser of the two evils.

In many ways, corrective discipline is like surgery. It is God's radical way of ridding the church of impurities. As we have already seen in the previous chapter, the foundation of church discipline is preventive. This, however, will not always be adequate. The church is not only composed of fallen human beings, it is also constantly under attack. We should not be surprised, therefore, when some members of the church fall into different kinds of sinful behaviour. It is at this point that corrective discipline becomes a necessity. Its purpose is to deal with specific issues and bring them to closure.

Which sins should be disciplined?

Before we look at the mechanics of corrective discipline, we need to give some thought to which kinds of sins necessitate it. This should not be some random process; rather, the leadership of a church should apply measured discipline to deal with specific problems as they arise. These problems should also be of sufficient severity to necessitate action. After all, if every kind of sin were to require discipline, every church member would perpetually be disciplined, for none of us is perfect. All too often, churches have fallen into the trap of pettiness, jumping on people for doing very little. Such an approach leads to paranoia, suspicion, gossiping and a critical attitude towards one another. Given that church discipline exists to maintain harmony and community, this kind of approach is destructive and counterproductive.

Furthermore, any action taken against a church member should be proportionate. If someone has an itch, you scratch it; you don't hit it with a sledgehammer. Likewise, if someone in the church has stumbled or made a mistake, the issue should be dealt with with the minimum of fuss rather than causing a storm. More often than not, applying austere measures leads to more damage and hurt, whereas a firm but gentle approach tends to be much more effective.

It is interesting to note that the New Testament anticipated the need for corrective discipline and lists a number of sins which require action. It therefore provides us with a model which we can use. The sins mentioned that necessitate discipline could be divided into the following six categories:

INTER-MEMBERSHIP CONFLICT

The first of these categories consists of those sins which result from conflict between members of the church:

> If your brother sins against you, go and show him his fault, just between the two of you. If he listens to you, you have won your brother over. But if he will not listen, take one or two others along, so that 'every matter may be established by the testimony of two or three witnesses'. If he refuses to listen to them, tell it to the church; and if he refuses to listen even to the church, treat him as you would a pagan or a tax collector.
>
> Matt. 18:15–17

> I say this to shame you. Is it possible that there is nobody among you wise enough to judge a dispute between believers? But instead, one brother goes to law against another—and this in front of unbelievers!
>
> 1 Cor. 6:5–6

Not all conflicts will be about the same kinds of issues, and likewise, not every conflict will be of the same severity. In the case in 1 Corinthians 6, the disagreement between the two church members was over an issue which appears to have been fairly insignificant. Moreover, those involved took the issue too far, even to the point of involving the legal process. Paul was clearly unhappy about this in principle and felt that the whole thing could have been resolved without it becoming a crisis.

In Matthew 18, however, the issue involved a real offence which one member had committed against another, not just a disagreement between them. This required dealing with, though Jesus again called for the parties concerned to be cautious about inflaming the situation. Action, said Jesus, should begin in a small way and only escalate if necessary.

Whatever the reasons for conflicts between church members, the reality is that they can become serious and can disrupt the church. Consequently, they will sometimes require intervention from church leaders and the application of corrective discipline.

INAPPROPRIATE SOCIAL BEHAVIOUR

A second category that necessitates discipline is the general area of inappropriate social behaviour. Within any given society, there are norms of behaviour that are considered appropriate. Needless to say, if Christians do not conform to this basic standard, they risk being bad examples to their non-Christian peers. Given that the reputation of the church is at stake, the church leadership has a responsibility to act in such a situation if it becomes potentially embarrassing. An example of this is found in 2 Thessalonians 3:6–14:

> In the name of the Lord Jesus Christ, we command you, brothers, to keep away from every brother who is idle and does not live according to the teaching you received from us. For you yourselves know how you ought to follow our example. We were not idle when we were with you, nor did we eat anyone's food without paying for it. On the contrary, we worked night and day, labouring and toiling so that we would not be a burden to any of you. We did this, not because we do not have the right to such help, but in order to make ourselves a model for you to follow. For even when we were with you, we gave you this rule: 'If a man will not work, he shall not eat.'

> We hear that some among you are idle. They are not busy; they are busybodies. Such people we command and urge in the Lord Jesus Christ to settle down and earn the bread they eat. And as for you, brothers, never tire of doing what is right.

> If anyone does not obey our instruction in this letter, take special note of him. Do not associate with him, in order that he may feel ashamed.

Here some Christians were being lazy and living off the generosity of their fellow Christians. Paul condemns this 'sponging' and demands a return to work.

It is not hard to imagine situations where Christians who behave inappropriately today might need some advice or correction. In one church I know, there was a situation where a husband was repeatedly verbally abusive and unkind to his wife. They were both church members and the elders were justifiably concerned, not least because his unpleasant attitude to his wife was well known to both neighbours and work colleagues. Given this situation, and the injustice done to the wife, the elders felt the need to visit and admonish the man to behave in a more Christlike manner in his home. The timely word was just what the situation required, as well as being faithful to biblical practice.

Unspiritual behaviour

As well as inappropriate social behaviour, there is a category of offence that relates to general unspiritual behaviour. Within any church, there is a basic level of behaviour that is acceptable and each member is expected to be a good and positive influence within the life of the church. If someone fails to do so and has a negative effect on the church, he or she should be dealt with accordingly.

When Paul wrote to Titus he raised this issue:

> This is a trustworthy saying. And I want you to stress these things, so that those who have trusted in God may be careful to devote themselves to doing what is good. These things are excellent and profitable for everyone.
>
> But avoid foolish controversies and genealogies and

arguments and quarrels about the law, because these are unprofitable and useless. Warn a divisive person once, and then warn him a second time. After that, have nothing to do with him. You may be sure that such a man is warped and sinful; he is self-condemned.

Titus 3:8–11

Within the church, there were people who were getting bogged down with foolish ideas and arguing for them. This was unhelpful within the church context and there was a danger of people having their attention diverted from focusing on what was important to focusing on issues that were insignificant. Paul called upon Titus to take action and discipline those people who were acting in this way.

This exact situation happened in a church at which I frequently preach. One of the members of the fellowship was an argumentative person who had very fixed opinions. His strength of conviction was not in itself a problem; his constant need to argue and debate, however, was. In house groups, he would dominate the discussion and frequently be rude to other members of the group. On one occasion, when his host, who was the house-group leader, tried to counter him on an issue, he quickly dismissed him as a 'compromiser' and questioned his spiritual integrity. As time went on, many church members got hurt by the sharp comments made to them, and several visiting preachers, including myself, were harangued in an inappropriate way after having delivered our messages. Finally, one of the elders was sent to speak to him and did so, graciously and gently, but nevertheless in a way that left the man in no doubt that he needed to change his ways and be kinder to his fellow Christians.

UNDERMINING LEADERSHIP

Another category which requires the application of disciplinary procedures is that of opposing or undermining the leadership of a church. This mostly happens in a covert way but it is a serious issue. The authority of an elder does not come from any rank which he possesses, but rather from God. That is not to say that all leaders are faultless or that they have the authority to rule in some kind of autocratic way. However, leadership does need to be respected as something that God has instituted.

That being the case, anyone who attempts to undermine the authority of the leaders of a church is not just opposing men, but ultimately opposing God.

Paul experienced this kind of opposition in his ministry. In 1 Timothy 1:20, he referred to Hymenaeus and Alexander: 'Among them are Hymenaeus and Alexander, whom I have handed over to Satan to be taught not to blaspheme.' We are not told exactly what they did, but clearly they were opposing the ministry that Paul was carrying out. Later on, in 2 Timothy 4:14–15, Paul mentions Alexander once more: 'Alexander the metalworker did me a great deal of harm. The Lord will repay him for what he has done. You too should be on your guard against him, because he strongly opposed our message.' We are not unreasonable in assuming that this Alexander is the same person Paul referred to in his first epistle to Timothy. On this second occasion, Paul was more explicit in telling us that Alexander had opposed the apostle's message and therefore did a great deal of harm. Here Paul called for action so that the wrongdoing could be corrected.

The reality is that, without a leadership structure in place, the church will end up in chaos. Though human leadership is by its very nature fallible, it is nevertheless necessary, and the integrity of a church's leadership structure must be maintained. If there are people within a church who deliberately set out to undermine the leadership, they must be dealt with.

Gross moral sins
A fifth category of sins that merit discipline consists of gross

moral sins. It goes without saying that action needs to be taken when church members offend in this way. The church's reputation is at stake and the church needs to be seen to be holy. Moreover, as repentance is at the heart of the Christian gospel, it would be very strange if the church were to turn a blind eye to lifestyles that are outside the moral boundaries that God has set.

It is hard to believe that such sins can actually occur within a church, but Paul's clear warnings indicate that they do. In 1 Corinthians 5:1–13 and 2 Corinthians 12:21 he lists some sins which believers should avoid:

> It is actually reported that there is sexual immorality among you, and of a kind that does not occur even among pagans: A man has his father's wife. And you are proud! Shouldn't you rather have been filled with grief and have put out of your fellowship the man who did this? Even though I am not physically present, I am with you in spirit. And I have already passed judgment on the one who did this, just as if I were present. When you are assembled in the name of our Lord Jesus and I am with you in spirit, and the power of our Lord Jesus is present, hand this man over to Satan, so that the sinful nature may be destroyed and his spirit saved on the day of the Lord.

> Your boasting is not good. Don't you know that a little yeast works through the whole batch of dough? Get rid of the old yeast that you may be a new batch without yeast—as you really are. For Christ, our Passover lamb, has been sacrificed. Therefore let us keep the Festival, not with the old yeast, the yeast of malice and wickedness, but with bread without yeast, the bread of sincerity and truth.

> I have written you in my letter not to associate with

sexually immoral people—not at all meaning the people of this world who are immoral, or the greedy and swindlers, or idolaters. In that case you would have to leave this world. But now I am writing you that you must not associate with anyone who calls himself a brother but is sexually immoral or greedy, an idolater or a slanderer, a drunkard or a swindler. With such a man do not even eat.

What business is it of mine to judge those outside the church? Are you not to judge those inside? God will judge those outside. 'Expel the wicked man from among you'

1 Cor. 5:1–13

I am afraid that when I come again my God will humble me before you, and I will be grieved over many who have sinned earlier and have not repented of the impurity, sexual sin and debauchery in which they have indulged

2 Cor. 12:21

The sins listed here include such evils as incest, greed, idolatry, drunkenness and robbery. Anyone found guilty of any of these things should be disciplined by the church in order to keep it pure.

Incredibly, however, in the present moral climate it is sometimes difficult to get a person to realize that what he or she is doing is wrong. In a situation with which I was recently involved, a church member was taken to task for having an affair with a neighbour. What made the situation even more painful was that her husband and children were also church members and were obviously deeply affected and embarrassed by what was happening. When the leaders of the church confronted her, she denied that she was doing anything wrong. Indeed, she stated that marrying her husband was a mistake and that the man with whom she was having an affair was really the person she should have married; consequently, this relationship was part of God's will for her. Clearly, such situations require a decisive response from the church.

HERETICS

A final category of sin for which a person should be disciplined is that of heresy: people who are guilty of peddling false doctrine. Correct doctrine is an essential component of church life. In Acts 2, as Luke describes for us the activities of the early church, he notes that the Christians devoted themselves to the apostles' doctrine: 'They devoted themselves to the apostles' teaching and to the fellowship, to the breaking of bread and to prayer' (v. 42). Truth is important and especially as it relates to what God has revealed to us through his Word. If any Christian, therefore, takes the truth of God's Word and distorts it so that what is conveyed is false, a great offence has been caused.

The New Testament is full of challenges to contend for the truth and reject falsehood. The epistle of Jude is one of the books which denounce this kind of sin most stridently (see vv. 16–19). In such cases, the elders, who have a role in guarding the theological integrity of the church, should respond to the falsehood with vigour.

A big issue

Given the above list, it must be emphasized that the business of church discipline is one to which a great deal of thought should be given. Ultimately, it is the responsibility of church leaders to ensure that the church is living up to God's expectation of it. When a church fails, its leaders must give some account of how they have led the church. This is an onerous task, but such is the importance of the church in the eyes of God! In John's Gospel, Jesus entered the temple and cleared out the people who had turned this sacred area into a marketplace (John 2:13–17). His zeal for the house of God consumed him. In 1 Corinthians 11, Paul gives the Christians in Corinth some instructions about how they should conduct themselves in church. He begins in verse 1 by telling them, 'Follow my example, as I follow the example of Christ.' In the same way that Christ had a concern about the dignity and integrity of the house of God, we should have a concern about the church which is God's holy temple. This desire should motivate church leaders to keep order within the church and use the tool of discipline when necessary.

The practicalities of doing this are, of course, easier stated than carried out. Indeed, church leaders need to have a range of qualities that enable them to do this successfully:

- good observation skills, so as to be aware when problems arise within the church
- pastoral hearts that will enable them to deal compassionately with difficult situations
- spiritual depth, not only so that they can distinguish between good and bad behaviour, but also so that they can have the moral authority to take action
- courage. Confronting sin and applying discipline is never an easy thing. The easy way out is to ignore the sin and take the ostrich approach, with heads buried in the sand. This, however, will never lead to a better and purer church, so courage is required for action to be taken.

Something to ponder

At this point, we need to look at the big picture. There can be little doubt that both preventive and corrective forms of discipline are necessary, and it should also be clear that God expects his church to serve him well. There are, however, some key words that will help us apply the issue of discipline in an appropriate way:

REALISM

We would all love to live in a world where Christians were perfect and temptation did not exist. It would be wonderful if our lives were so uncomplicated that every choice we made was simple and the demarcation between right and wrong was brilliantly clear. However, this is simply not the kind of world in which we live. Our world is fallen and full of complications. People find themselves wrapped up in intractable problems where solutions are almost impossible to find. It is in this context that churches have to operate.

This has a bearing on church discipline. As we try to steer members of our churches in the right direction and coach them to achieve excellence in their spiritual lives, we need to begin by recognizing where they are coming from. There is always a context within which they operate and this has to be borne in mind when the issue of discipline is raised. This is not to say that we should excuse sin simply because someone's life is difficult; it does mean, however, that we need to see a person's actions against the background of his or her life's experience and present circumstances.

Samantha was typical of this. She was a new Christian who began regularly attending an evangelical church and decided that she wanted to get baptized and become a member. The pastor of her church led her through a baptismal and membership class, during which time she began a relationship with a non-Christian man called Geoff. The situation was further complicated by the fact that Samantha was already married to her husband Dave. Though she was not yet a church member, the leadership team of her church nevertheless felt that they had to act and do something about this undesirable situation.

On one level, it would have been perfectly understandable if the leadership of the church banned Samantha from participating in communion and also refused to baptize her until she got her life sorted out. They would also have reasonably been able to demand that she break off the relationship which she had just begun. This would have been straightforward and a fairly clean solution. However, there was an important context to bear in mind in all of this. To begin with, both Samantha and her husband Dave were heroin addicts, although Samantha had managed, with a great deal of help, to come off her addiction. Shortly after they got married, Dave became very abusive, to the point where Samantha at times feared for her life. He also made her work as a prostitute so that she could pay for their drug habits. It was while Dave was spending a short time in prison that Samantha got involved with a close friend she had known most of her life, Geoff, and ended up having a baby son called Ben with him. The friendship between them ended once Dave came out of prison.

Shortly before her conversion, Samantha left Dave, not least because she felt that she would not be able to live a life free from drugs if she stayed with him. It was at this point that she was converted and began attending church. In time, her boyfriend Geoff came back onto the scene and wanted to be a good father to their son Ben. Geoff was a very genuine person and their relationship appeared to have the potential to last.

The church leaders had a very difficult decision to make. Should they take decisive action in order to safeguard the purity of the church, or should they show compassion and understanding to a needy and hurting person? Furthermore, there was the issue of three-year-old-son Ben. Geoff was the real father and wanted to play the role of father and husband. Whatever the decision, it was clear that the overall context had to be taken into consideration and that a superficial response was not the right thing.

DAMAGE LIMITATION

Once we recognize the need for realism, we should also countenance the concept of damage limitation. Given that life can be so very complex, we would be foolish if we thought that there is always a good solution to a problem. Often it is more a case of choosing the solution that causes the least amount of damage.

In one situation, a divorcee who was a member of a church decided to get married again to someone else within the church. Though both of them were Christians, the leaders of the church were a little uncertain about the situation, not least because it was hard to find the real cause for the breakdown of the first marriage. Their church policy was that divorcees were free to remarry if they had been abandoned by their partners or if their previous partners had been unfaithful to them. In this case, however, the fault was not entirely clear.

This complex situation left them uncertain as to how to progress. However, there were a number of considerations on which they had to reflect. Firstly, although the Bible states that God hates divorce and that there are only certain conditions under which remarriage is possible, in this case there was a new relationship that would nevertheless almost certainly continue. Furthermore, if the leaders were to clamp down hard on the new couple, they might be in danger either of discouraging them or of driving them away from church altogether. In such a scenario, there is no perfect solution; the damage has been done and the situation is difficult. The question was: What would be the least damaging way forward? Some might argue that thinking in this way is, in itself, a compromise and that we need to apply biblical principles rigidly. While it is undoubtedly true that biblical principles need to be applied, in the absence of a perfect or even good solution, the church simply needs to find the next best thing to do.

EVIDENCE

It is a huge mistake to carry out any disciplinary procedure against someone unless it is absolutely clear that that person is in the wrong. According to the legal system of most Western countries, a person is innocent until proved guilty. It is reasonable to expect the same standard of justice in church life. Whether this evidence comes from the testimony of credible witnesses or the admission of the perpetrator, there must be no doubt that the person concerned has been at fault. Even if this process takes time in order for a sufficient body of evidence to be amassed, it is surely better to wait rather than act hastily.

FLEXIBILITY

Just as people come in different shapes and sizes, so too do their problems and issues. It would therefore be foolish to have a one-size-fits-all approach to how we deal with them. Robert and Hillary are good examples of this. Though they are man and wife, they are completely different people who have both stumbled at different times in their Christian lives. Though they were guilty of much the same thing, their way of dealing with failure differed. They had both lived colourful lives prior to their conversions and for some time afterwards they periodically involved themselves in the clubbing scene, which for them also involved taking recreational drugs. Hillary felt enormously guilty and actually asked her pastor if she could talk to him. With an open heart, she confided in him, telling him of her struggle with drugs. For her, all it took was some firm but gentle advice, and the problem was solved.

Robert, on the other hand, proved much more difficult. Initially, he denied that there was anything wrong, even when challenged. Then, when the evidence began to mount and the pastor came to have a word with him about his behaviour, he turned belligerent. This led to a battle of wills. Given the context, the pastor was wise enough not to draw a line in the sand too quickly. He asked Robert to consider some mentoring and perhaps even counselling. As an interim measure, the pastor asked Robert not to continue as a youth leader in the church, something that Robert very much enjoyed. He did not, however, stop Robert from taking part in communion. This meant that he could still enjoy fellowship and the possibility of spiritual growth, but while constantly being reminded of the wrong choices he was making.

As time went on, this embargo had its effect. Robert realized the error of his ways and that, if he was not walking closely with God, he could not be a positive influence on the young people of the church for whom he had a real burden. Happily, he and Hillary are at the time of writing completely free of any drug use. In both cases, the flexibility demonstrated by the pastor proved to be an effective way forward.

HUMILITY

This is crucial, because there is nothing more heartbreaking than being chastised by someone who has a proud or smug demeanour. Whether we like it or not, the reality is that human personalities become an issue in church disciplinary situations. Those being censured will, quite naturally, be very observant of the way in which they are being treated. If those carrying out the censure are not seen to be humble and gentle, their actions will only cause deep hurt rather than helping the fallen Christian. This, of course, is utterly counterproductive.

Christians can often have a holier-than-thou attitude that does not seem far removed from the self-righteousness of the Pharisees. In truth, we are all capable of falling into sin or even deliberately doing things of which we know God disapproves. Therefore, as we carry out church discipline, we should do so with the humility of those who realize their own weaknesses and fallibility and with a compassion for the person who has stumbled. After all, as the adage says, 'There but for the grace of God go I'.

GRACE

It is interesting to observe Jesus' ministry and to note his anger in relation to the heartless and rigid attitude of the Pharisees (Mark 3:1–6; John 7:23–24). Jesus was not soft on sin, but he recognized that a legalistic and inflexible attitude to the complexities of fallen humanity is not always good. Jesus hated sin yet loved the sinner, and demonstrated God's grace in so many different settings. While church discipline does need to be carried out, there must be a recognition that we serve a Master who is gracious, and this must temper our approach.

DISCERNMENT

It is also important to think about the direction in which the fallen church member is going. Clearly, if there is no evidence of repentance, disciplinary procedures need to be applied. However, if there has been genuine repentance and the person has a real desire to get back to a close relationship with God, this must be taken into consideration. Unless the offence which has been committed has wider ramifications, one could argue that it would be unhelpful to exercise any church discipline. A proactive approach to discipleship might prove to be better. Of course, the church does need to be seen to be doing the right thing and to act when sin is present. If the offence is serious, and especially if it has become well known or perhaps others have been affected by it, some sort of action is appropriate. However, wisdom is needed, and the attitude of the individual concerned is highly significant.

FORGIVENESS

We should always remember that the ultimate goal of church discipline is the spiritual restoration of the individual who has fallen. This will require a long-sighted approach: we need to ask questions about how the disciplinary procedures will contribute to the person being rehabilitated. It will also require forgiveness on the part of the church members. If forgiveness is not forthcoming, it is hard to see how a fallen brother or sister can be restored. Forgiveness should therefore be something we try to offer as a community.

Putting it into practice

We now come to the issue of what kind of corrective discipline is available to churches. In this we need to remember that we are actually giving God's verdict on the situation concerned and that we have no authority of our own. Rather, the entire congregation falls under the authority of God and his will as expressed in the Bible. Our role is to carry out God's wishes within the Christian community. This is a daunting responsibility and one that requires great care, for our purpose is not to vent our dislike of the fallen member but to ensure that God's church is purified and the wayward church member brought into conformity with God's will once more. The endgame is always restoration and ongoing nurture. That being the case, we need to reflect carefully on the rationale behind church discipline.

New Testament discipline

Even a cursory glance of disciplinary procedures in the New Testament reveals a degree of complexity. Clearly, a simplistic approach will never deal adequately with the complexities of human existence. There is variety within the New Testament procedures, not only in terms of their severity, but also in relation to methodology.

Some years ago, I was in Croatia on a mission team. Our main purpose was to do some evangelism and Bible teaching, but we also wanted to do some practical work which would help believers in this war-torn land to get their lives back together again. One particular Christian leader was dismantling his damaged house so that he could build another one. As we set to work to help on this task, we quickly recognized that we needed a wide range of tools to do the job. Small hammers were needed to knock out the remaining broken glass from the house windows, but when we got to the brickwork and the concrete foundations, these small hammers were utterly unless. For those jobs, we needed to use heavy sledgehammers. Of course, the opposite was also true: if my job was only to knock out the broken pieces of glass from a window frame, and I used a sledgehammer to do it, I would exhaust myself but not do an effective job.

The same applies when it comes to church discipline, and that is why the process is varied and set in stages. New Testament discipline is not a one-size-fits-all umbrella; rather, we are required to think clearly and make judgements about which form of discipline is appropriate for a particular case, and when to move from one stage of the disciplinary process to the next. The picture that emerges is of a multi-stage process that prevents any rushed judgements or unnecessary escalations.

Challenging one another

The first stage in the process of discipline is that of personal admonition. In order to understand this stage properly, we need to remind ourselves of the responsibilities of every church member. We noted in Chapter 2 that the New Testament teaches a priesthood of all believers and that individual Christians have a duty to correct wrong behaviour when they see it occurring. This kind of correction falls into two categories: the category of general offence and the category of personal offence. The former is mentioned is Galatians 6:1: 'Brothers, if someone is caught in a sin, you who are spiritual should restore him gently. But watch yourself, or you also may be tempted.' Here Paul commands believers to speak out when they see a fellow Christian sinning so that that person can be restored. Likewise, in 1 Thessalonians 5:14, he urges church members to 'warn those who are idle, encourage the timid, help the weak …' In these cases, a quiet but firm word in the ear is necessary; clearly, this is something that should not come to public attention. The idea is that a gentle rebuke should be sufficient to deal with the situation.

Not long before writing this, it came to my attention that a Christian friend of mine was accessing inappropriate websites.

I discovered this because we shared the same computer at a library we both frequented. Although he was not a member of my church, I nevertheless felt I had to say something because he was, after all, my brother in Christ. However, at this stage I deemed it unnecessary to involve anyone from his church. I spoke to him one day over coffee and suggested to him that, unless he was more careful about what he saw and what he allowed his mind to dwell on, his spiritual development would be greatly impaired. He received the rebuke with a humble and repentant spirit and thanked me for my advice. We prayed together as we finished our conversation, and have done the same many times since. At no point did he feel he was being 'got at' by me; he fully recognized that what I said came from a deep concern for him. As far as I know, he has never sinned in this way again and our friendship has only increased. It seems to me that this is the kind of thing Paul had in mind in Galatians 6 and 1 Thessalonians 5, and it can be a very effective form of corrective discipline.

The second category is mentioned in Matthew 18:15: 'If your brother sins against you, go and show him his fault, just between the two of you. If he listens to you, you have won your brother over.' This involves a Christian who has been offended by another believer going to that person and dealing with the issue. This is slightly more difficult, as there will inevitably be some tension between the two people involved. However, it is an important principle to bear in mind. So often, when difficulties arise between Christians, the situation is exacerbated as other people are brought into the argument.

As a church leader, I have often been approached by people in my church who are angry about fellow church members and want me to deal with the issues. Often, those who have made them angry are not even aware that they have caused any hurt, and sometimes, when they find out the hurt they have caused, they are devastated. Experience has taught me to ask those who approach me one simple question: 'Have you talked to that person and told him/her what you feel?'

Jesus demonstrated great practical wisdom in telling the offended person to go alone to the offender and talk about the issue. There are four reasons why this is a good idea:

- The more people who are involved in the argument, the more complicated it will get. People will inevitably take sides and will often inflame the debate by pouring more fuel on the fire.
- When two Christians actually deal with a difficulty and talk it out, their relationship is often strengthened.
- When an issue is dealt with in this personal way, the offender can see clearly the effect of his or her actions and the offended party can also see clearly any remorse that is there.
- These simple face-to-face talks enable both parties to have their say and then move on from the issue.

Needless to say, these kinds of confrontations will only work if the two people involved approach their meeting in a mature and spiritual manner. If the offended party simply wants to vent his or her frustration and use the meeting as a way of expressing disdain for the other person, a clash will result. Likewise, if the offender becomes defensive and will not admit that a wrong has been committed either intentionally or unintentionally, the discussions will be fruitless. Worse still, if the offender becomes indignant and begins to make counter-accusations, the situation will rapidly deteriorate. It seems reasonable, therefore, that this kind of conflict resolution should be taught in the teaching programme of the church, and church members should be encouraged to hear Jesus' words and obey them in a constructive way.

Going with a witness
It would be wonderful to think that every issue could simply be

solved by carrying out a one-to-one form of discipline. None of us, however, comes from a perfect church, and neither are we perfect Christians. Moreover, there are also offences that are of such a serious nature that a mere word in the ear is not appropriate. For this reason, there are further stages in the disciplinary process.

It was Jesus himself who described what should happen if the initial word of correction didn't work. In Matthew 18:16–17, he stated that, if the offender 'will not listen, take one or two others along, so that "every matter may be established by the testimony of two or three witnesses." If he refuses to listen to them, tell it to the church; and if he refuses to listen even to the church, treat him as you would a pagan or a tax collector.'

A number of things can be extrapolated from this reference. Firstly, Jesus was concerned that any action taken should be carried out in a calm and measured way. A person's refusal to repent should not result in immediate action on behalf of the whole church and may not even require the involvement of church leaders. Rather, there should be an interim stage of taking some witnesses.

Secondly, there is an expectation that, whatever action is taken, there should be some evidence of remorse or repentance on behalf of the offender. In other words, discipline is not just about telling someone off; rather, it is about finding resolution to the satisfaction of all concerned. Clearly, the person who has sinned should be restored, but the person who has been sinned against should also be satisfied that there is evidence of contrition. Given that the church is a family, personal relationships are of utmost importance.

Thirdly, the purpose of taking along a couple of witnesses is twofold. Initially, they provide objective input to the argument, but they also add some moral weight which will encourage resolution. It goes without saying that the witnesses should be impartial and spiritually discerning. They need to listen carefully to both sides and bring a considered response.

Getting the church involved

Jesus' statement suggests that, when the bringing of a witness does not lead to resolution, the involvement of the whole believing community becomes necessary.

The New Testament never tires of describing the church in terms of community. The church is a body that stands together and makes unified decisions. Therefore, it is assumed that, if any major disciplinary process takes place, the church needs to be not only aware of what is happening, but also involved in the process. As we will see from some of the Pauline passages that deal with the issue of discipline, the church's role is a crucial one and involves every member.

At this point, a number of observations should be made. Firstly, the model of church will affect the way in which the church is told. Some churches have an intimate feel about them and it may be appropriate to talk openly about the issue during a church service. In other churches, it may be better to deal with the issue in the context of a house group, or even for the leaders to visit every member and discuss the issue personally. Sometimes, the injunction 'tell it to the church' may appropriately be carried out simply by putting it on the agenda of the leadership meeting. However, whichever method is used, the teaching of Jesus is clear: it is an issue for the church as a body, not just for the leadership of the church.

Secondly, it goes without saying that escalating the matter to this stage should not be done hurriedly. Every opportunity should be given to allow the fallen church member to repent and relationships to be restored. Personally, I would rather take witnesses several times, in the hope that the matter would be resolved, before going on to involve the whole church. With the best will in the world, once the whole church is aware of an issue, it will never be forgotten. This, in turn, may make it very difficult for the disciplined member to re-establish him- or herself within the community. Telling it to the church should therefore be seen as a last resort when everything else has failed.

Thirdly, every effort must be made to suppress gossip and backbiting. Church members are not involved in the issue so that they can pass judgement on the fallen person; rather, they are to encourage, love and draw that person back into full life in the Christian community. That being the case, their approach to the person concerned is crucial. It may well be that Jesus anticipated that church members would individually spend time with the person involved and that the weight of their corporate response would have an impact. Certainly, if church relationships are strong and members are committed to promoting one another's spiritual excellence, the impact of such a move will be profound. The members can demonstrate to the fallen individual just how important being part of a Christian family can be.

The final court of appeal

If all the previous steps have been taken and the person involved has still not repented, there remains one final act of discipline, namely, exclusion from the community. In 1 Corinthians 5:1–5, Paul describes this final eventuality:

> It is actually reported that there is sexual immorality among you, and of a kind that does not occur even among pagans: A man has his father's wife. And you are proud! Shouldn't you rather have been filled with grief and have put out of your fellowship the man who did this? Even though I am not physically present, I am with you in spirit. And I have already passed judgment on the one who did this, just as if I were present. When you are assembled in the name of our Lord Jesus and I am with you in spirit, and the power of our Lord Jesus is present, hand this man over to Satan, so that the

sinful nature may be destroyed and his spirit saved on the day of the Lord.

The particular issue which is being dealt with is one of sexual immorality. Reading between the lines in 1 Corinthians 5, there are a number of inferences that can be drawn. Firstly, it seems that the sin mentioned has been investigated and the person's guilt is unquestioned. Presumably, the leaders who had overall responsibility for the spiritual wellbeing of the church had done this. The idea of careful investigation is mentioned again in 1 Timothy 5:19, where Paul suggests that a case is only valid if clear evidence is presented by two or three witnesses. Guilt needs to be proved beyond any doubt. In the Corinthians 5 case, there was already a public scandal, which further emphasized the need for action.

A second inference is that the person concerned was already aware that his lifestyle was unacceptable but he was unwilling to change. Thirdly, the church was as lax as the individual in dealing with the issue. Paul's concern was therefore not just about the man in question and his sin, but also about the church's inability to keep its house in order. His call was for decisive action, with the removal from fellowship of the offending member.

It is at this point that we see the role which the church as a community plays in the disciplinary procedure. The leaders were to supervise the discipline, but it was the church as a whole that was to carry it out. Not only was the man to be denied fellowship within the church, but also all the members were effectively to treat him as an outcast. He was to be denied the benefits of being part of a community of faith.

Church membership is a responsibility as well as a privilege. As members of a church, we have a right to expect the love, interest and support of our fellow Christians. In addition, we have the privilege of an intimate relationship with God through his church. Of course, we can and must enjoy a relationship with God as individuals. But we must never allow our Western individualism to detract from the fact that God works in community and that he meets with his people in a special way in community.

When we come together as church, God is there in a particular sense. It is here that the church as a whole takes part in the disciplinary procedure. The person being disciplined is denied any access to church fellowship and the rights of family membership. Church members are not obliged to demonstrate the love, concern and interest that they owe to fellow community members. Indeed, Paul makes it clear to the Corinthians that they should make a point of not doing so, in order that the disciplinary procedure can be truly effective. Any church member who breaks rank will nullify the power of the exclusion.

An interesting point to note from 1 Corinthians 5 is that the person being removed from church fellowship is being 'handed over to Satan'. This is a highly emotive and graphic term that Paul is using and it is something that he does not expand upon. However, it is not unreasonable to suggest that Paul is simply saying that, once a person is 'outside' church fellowship, he or she is in the realm of Satan. The church functions as a spiritual sanctuary and we as Christians draw strength from one another which equips us for facing the devil. Those who openly live sinful lives and experience exclusion will not be able to avail themselves of this privilege.

On the face of it, this seems a harsh approach. However, we need to remind ourselves that, in the particular case Paul was dealing with in 1 Corinthians 5, the man concerned was wilfully living a sinful life and refused to repent, even though he knew it would have been the right thing to do. Sin is a dangerous and insidious thing, especially when it is consciously committed, and we as Christians should be concerned that our sinful environment does not affect us so much that we do not recognize the seriousness of sin when it occurs in our midst. If we are not careful, we can become sentimental and falsely compassionate towards people who have fallen and, in doing so, turn a blind eye to the wrong they have done.

I am not saying for a moment that compassion has no part to play: it does, and in all that we do we should demonstrate it. When we discipline people, we should do so with aching hearts and tears in our eyes. However, sin is sin, and it is not an act of kindness to pretend otherwise. Every parent knows that love and anger are not incompatible. Indeed, the parent who cares nothing for the discipline of a child is a parent who cares nothing for the child. When Christians do wrong and refuse to repent, they damage themselves, the church and the credibility of the gospel. With all that is at stake, the church must take the pathway of tough love and exercise whatever disciplinary measures are required, even if it means cutting someone off from the church's Christian family.

Even at this stage in the process of discipline, those involved should not lose hope of the eventual restoration of the individual, for even exclusion from the community is for the purpose of bringing the fallen member back into full community life once more. Of course, the effectiveness of this final form of discipline will be entirely contingent on the quality of relationships within the church. I know of one individual who was excommunicated but, as his church was not a warm and friendly place, he did not miss it. This made the discipline utterly ineffective and did nothing to restore him to a right relationship with God. The best way to ensure that discipline is effective is to build a strong and loving community to which all of its members will want to commit themselves.

The endgame

It would be wrong to suggest that, once all of these things have been carried out, our job of disciplining a person is over.

On the contrary, it is only half done. This is because church discipline includes the restoration of the individual. There is a debate raging in the prison service today about the purpose of custodial sentences. Are they a punishment, a re-education or both? When it comes to church discipline, there is an element of punishment, but it is also designed to teach Christians how to live and to excel spiritually. Clearly, therefore, it is not enough just to impose a sanction on a fallen church member; we also need to work towards that person's reconciliation and normal fellowship once more with his or her Christian family. Anything less, and the process has failed.

The New Testament does not actually indicate what must be done in order to bring someone back into fellowship within the church; it merely assumes that this is what should be done. There is also a presumption that the different stages of discipline will be a powerful incentive to come back into a living relationship with Jesus Christ and the church family once more. However, some practical things can be done to facilitate any restoration:

- When the disciplinary procedure is being carried out, make it clear to the person concerned that he or she will be welcomed back following repentance. More than that, emphasize that the church as a body will feel the loss of that person's absence and will actively be praying for restoration. If the person has felt loved and cared for by fellow church members, this experience will give him or her confidence to believe that there will be a genuine welcome back.
- Educate the church members as a whole as to their responsibilities. As we have already noted, they have a role in holding rank and making the exclusion a genuine one. But, equally, they have a role in welcoming back anyone who returns to the sanctuary of the church. This is an exceedingly important yet difficult thing to do. It is

difficult because it is always a slightly awkward situation when someone who has fallen away returns. The fallen individual may have caused deep hurts and therefore there is a need to be forgiving and compassionate. The person may feel nervous and uncomfortable about meeting people he or she has let down. Often when someone returns to church for the first time, the atmosphere can be tense. However, the importance of this task is self-evident. We must recognize that it is exceptionally difficult to come back to a church once you have been disciplined by it. Only when the members are genuinely welcoming and embracing can this restoration be made complete.

Punitive discipline

At this point, another issue requires attention. The models of church discipline that we have already mentioned deal only with a limited number of situations. The private word of rebuke and even the word of rebuke in the presence of witnesses relate only to sins of a less serious nature. These forms of discipline would be appropriate if, for example, someone were to be guilty of gossip, dishonesty or the slandering of fellow believers. The exclusion of a church member from Christian fellowship would apply to a serious sin that has not been repented of. If, for example, a believer were to have an adulterous affair or become involved in an illegal activity, and were to refuse to repent, this form of discipline would be appropriate. The question remains, however, as to what should be done if someone commits a serious sin and *does* repent. Should that person still face a disciplinary procedure?

An example of a real situation may help to clarify the issue. Peter was a businessman who owned a successful small company. He was also a committed church member. Several other church members had business links with Peter and, consequently, when his business went through a difficult patch, they became aware of it. On several occasions, church members and, in particular, two of his elders gave him advice and tried to encourage him. He always thanked them for their concern but never talked very much about his company's problems.

Then his problems went from bad to worse. He went to see one of the elders and confessed that he had been involved in some illegal deals in an attempt to rescue the ailing business and that the police were conducting an investigation. Although his misdemeanours would probably not lead to a custodial sentence, there was every likelihood that he would be fined and that the business might be called into receivership. He was deeply apologetic and sincerely pleaded with this elder for forgiveness. He also told the elder that he had asked God for forgiveness and that he was determined to serve God in the future, no matter what the cost. A few days later, the police charged Peter, he subsequently received a substantial fine and the business was closed. To add to the complication, not only did Peter lose everything, but also some church members who had invested in his company also lost money. The question which the elders had to ask themselves was whether or not Peter should still be subject to church discipline.

This kind of issue is not easy to deal with because there are a number of factors which require consideration. Firstly, if repentance is deemed to be genuine, what value do we give to it? Would disciplining the person actually undermine the importance of repentance? Secondly, when someone is repentant and broken, would the further application of discipline actually damage that person spiritually and make it more difficult for him or her to come back into a living relationship with Christ? The complexity of these issues necessitates that each situation must be taken on its own merits and that sober judgement must be applied.

There are a number of other issues that need to be thought

about. Firstly, just because someone has repented, it does not necessarily follow that his or her contrition abrogates the need for discipline. To give a very general example from everyday life, let us suppose that someone were to steal something from a local shop and then, having been caught, he or she expressed extreme sorrow for the crime committed. The sorrow and repentance would not convince the police or prosecutor to drop the charges. The church, of course, is a very different place from the law courts, but the issue of justice is just the same. Even if a person is genuinely repentant, it does not necessarily follow that he or she does not require the application of justice.

Secondly, the reputation of the Christian church is also at stake. Of course, the church is not a repository of perfect people and neither should we expect that every member is free from personal difficulties. On the contrary, it is a place for sinners to find love and acceptance, as well as forgiveness. Nevertheless, if people within the church sin openly and then readily repent in the hope of avoiding disciplinary action, it can give the impression that sin does not really matter. All a person needs to do is express sorrow and all is forgiven! This kind of approach would not only encourage sinful lifestyles in the church, it would also send the wrong message to the community at large.

Thirdly, it is true in church life just as in life in general that you reap what you sow. If there is a pattern of behaviour that is destructive, it is reasonable to expect bad consequences. The fact that someone repents of a particular sin does not mean that there are no further lessons to be learned. The application of discipline could therefore be extremely positive, because it would remind the person that he or she cannot go on living like that. It would be a powerful deterrent and would give the person time to reflect on the seriousness of his or her actions.

In the final analysis, the leadership of a church needs to weigh up each situation individually and come to a decision that takes into consideration all the facts and bears in mind the long-term spiritual wellbeing of the person concerned, as well as the interests of the church community. The decision must reflect the need to preserve the purity of the church as well as to demonstrate a compassion for the fallen believer. This will never be an easy balance to achieve, but continuing or initiating discipline need not offset the balance.

Of course, the way in which the discipline is administered, and even the type of discipline used, will be different in the case of a repentant person from that in which the person did not repent. The church needs clearly to demonstrate the importance of repentance and the motives of the individual. For example, if someone is genuinely repentant, a simple rebuke and some intensive discipleship might suffice; if, on the other hand, he or she refuses to repent, the action taken would need to be much more stringent. This is the kind of tough love which keeps a church functioning properly.

Lessons from the school of hard knocks

Chapter 5

History should be written as philosophy.

—Voltaire

However hard we work at preserving the purity of the church, the fact remains that discipline will always be a hard task. It is a task that is further complicated by the reality that so many things can go wrong. There is a real sense in which we need continually to input into our church life the lessons we have learned from past experience. This is because we are, at best, failing people trying to be biblical about the way in which we conduct church life. It is also important to ground our theory in real life. In this chapter, in discussing some of the potential pitfalls, we will look at four real accounts of things that went wrong and then reflect on lessons that can be learned from them. Needless to say, the names are fictitious, but the situations and the people concerned were all too real.

The problem of escapees

Michael was a committed church member who greatly contributed to the life of his church. He was loved and appreciated, not least because he was very gifted. Then disaster struck and he had a brief affair. The elders came to see him to try to resolve the situation. Their first concern was pastoral, as this unfortunate event had implications for all the people involved in it. As they began to pick up the pieces from this event, they moved onto the issue of discipline. At no point in their discussions with Michael did he express any deep sense of shame or repentance. He did acknowledge that his actions were sinful, but he excused his mistake by saying that he simply fell because of weakness. At the same time, he told the elders that he felt that they were being intrusive and that his 'mistakes' were none of their business.

This situation was clearly unacceptable, so the elders decided that Michael should be prevented from taking part in the weekly communion service for a period of three months. They conveyed this to him and assured him that they still loved him, but felt that this action was necessary. In addition, they looked forward to the time when he would be back in full fellowship within the church and serving alongside his fellow Christians. Michael responded by simply leaving the church.

This is when the situation became more complicated. Just a couple of miles down the road was another evangelical church. As Michael knew some of the people there, he began to attend and, within a matter of weeks, he was brought into membership. The remarkable thing was that the leaders in his new church asked very few questions about his relationship with the church he had just left. They were just happy to have another person added to their membership list.

This situation was unfortunate, but also wrong for several reasons:

- The decision to accept Michael into membership in the new church without investigating the circumstances in which he was coming demonstrated scant regard for the universal church. Every local church needs to recognize that it forms part of a large body which includes every true believer throughout the world. If the leaders of the church in question had recognized this, they would have, at the very least, tried to establish why Michael had left and would have given serious consideration as to whether they should refuse him membership until he had resolved his differences with his previous church.
- Michael had sinned against God, not just the church. It was strange, therefore, that this second church should have so little concern for God's honour.
- The church's decision to accept him into membership communicated the message that no one ever needs to

face discipline. All a person needs to do is go to another church and all will be well.

- The church's decision did not do Michael any good. As we have already noted, discipline can actually contribute to our long-term spiritual health. Michael never actually faced any discipline, so he was in no position to grow as a result of its application.
- It merely delayed the inevitable: God's judgement. The reality is that Michael never came to a position of genuine repentance. He avoided getting there by changing his place of worship. God, however, is not so easily fooled and we should never feel that a crafty move like that will escape his omniscient gaze. The truth is that, one day, Michael will have to give account for his error.

It is clear that steps need to be taken to ensure that this kind of situation does not arise. In my own church, we are proactive in this area. If someone comes to our church from another in the hope of joining, we always interview that person carefully in order to establish the reasons for wanting to be a part of our church. On most occasions, the reasons are valid and justified. Some have joined because our church is geographically closer than the one from which they have came, others because our church offers something positive to them or their children which they are not able to get from their old church. This kind of transfer growth is not necessarily a bad thing. People need to be in a church where they feel comfortable and fulfilled and where they are able to contribute as well as grow. However, if people want to join us simply because they have fallen out with members in their previous churches, we are not prepared to accept them.

As well as interview the prospective new member, we make contact with the leaders of that person's previous church. On most occasions, the leaders of the other church express both appreciation for our policy and a willingness to commend the person concerned to our fellowship. However, if the leaders express grave reservations about the move or highlight some unresolved issue in their relationship with the person concerned, we go no further until the situation has been resolved to everyone's satisfaction. In this way, a person is not able to escape discipline in another church and find fellowship in our church. This position recognizes the importance and dignity of both the local and the universal church.

The problem of inconsistency

Robert was an elder in a large urban church. He was popular with church members and had a charismatic personality which made him a considerable asset to the church. Often, because of his considerable leadership abilities, issues of pastoral care and church discipline would be deferred to him by his fellow elders. These he handled well. He had one great weakness, however, and that was that he had his favourites, and everyone knew this. There were some people in the church that he was particularly friendly with, and others to whom he barely spoke. It never became a problem until an incident occurred that rocked the church.

A serious dispute arose between two of the young adults in the church. This couple had been dating for several months. Robert had never encouraged their relationship, not least because he liked Julie but did not like Simon. He always felt that Julie was too good for Simon and so, in his dealings with them, he poured caution on their flowering relationship. Simon did have a few issues in his life to contend with, but so did Julie. The chemistry between the three was complicated by the fact that Simon knew how Robert felt about him and disliked him in return, whereas Julie thought Robert was wonderful, and often told him so.

As the months rolled by, strains began to appear in the

relationship between Simon and Julie. It may have been that they were simply incompatible, but the strains turned to cracks and then a gaping wound because of the unkind way in which they treated each other. Eventually, they broke up and became embittered with each other. The fault lay on both sides equally, but while Robert was quick to visit and offer support for Julie, he barely paid any attention to Simon.

The feud became very ugly, with each party accusing the other of a multitude of offences and using these as a justification for slander. As others in the congregation took sides and the issue became bigger, the elders felt that something needed to be done. Robert was assigned the job of visiting the two and sorting out the problem. Wisely, he decided that what was required at this stage was nothing more than a stern rebuke. However, his rebuke to Simon was much more severe than the one he delivered to Julie, and he made it clear that he thought that Simon was the main culprit. His assessment, however, was wrong and coloured by his dislike of Simon and his fondness for Julie. They both knew that, as did all the onlookers within the church who became aware of what was going on.

The situation dramatically deteriorated. Simon felt aggrieved about the way in which he was being treated and reacted angrily. Robert, in turn, used this as justification to return with another elder to deliver an ultimatum: unless Simon repented and admitted his fault, he would be disciplined more severely. For Simon, this was the last straw. He left the church, not because of the hurt that had been caused by the beak-up of his relationship with Julie, or even because he was being rebuked, but because he was treated unjustly.

Clearly, impartiality is fundamental in the discipline of people in the church. There needs to be even-handedness in the way we treat everyone. We human beings are, by our very nature, inconsistent. We are not machines but flesh and blood with real feelings capable of being swayed. Given this danger, church leaders should make a point of analysing whether or not they show favouritism and dealing with it before they cause any damage. There also needs to be an inbuilt system of accountability so that no such problem arises. It is inevitable that there will be some people in our churches to whom we naturally warm and others with whom we struggle. We need to be particularly vigilant so that, when the need for discipline arises, our feelings do not impair our sound judgement.

The problem of pettiness

James is a young man from a non-Christian home who began to go to church as a result of the witness of some of his school friends. He became a Christian at the age of sixteen and was then baptized and brought into fellowship. He was different in many ways from most of the other young people in the church. They came, by and large, from middle-class backgrounds, were highly motivated at school and prided themselves on their upbringings. In most cases, their parents and grandparents were Christians, so they easily fitted into church life.

James, on the other hand, came from a working-class family with no Christian background. His father, a steel worker, had an alcohol problem and a complete disregard for the niceties of life. James had a big personality, he talked continually, was naturally very humorous and had a raucous laugh. He was also very loud, could often be crude, and lacked a sense of decorum. All of this came as a shock to the church, especially to parents, who were more than a little concerned about the influence he might have on their children.

Several of the young people in the church liked James and enjoyed his company. They could see that behind the larger-than-life exterior was a very genuine person with a heart of gold which actually made him quite vulnerable. The youth leader also liked him and could see that real spiritual growth was taking place in his life. He was wise enough to know that the occasional expletive that came from James's mouth was not a sign that he was a bad Christian, but rather that the previous influences on his life were still a real factor. What is more, he was able to distinguish the difference between symptoms of spiritual decay and issues such as James's occasional crudity, which were no more than a sign of social ineptitude.

The problem James faced was that not everyone in the church had such a benevolent attitude towards him. Indeed, the majority of the elders did not like him and their attitude towards him was shared by most of the congregation. Then came the inevitable: James fell in love with one of the girls in the church and they began dating. Her parents were very unhappy about this, as was her uncle, who was one of the elders. They feared that James would lead the girl astray, though, in truth, there was nothing in his behaviour to indicate this, as he was actually growing in his Christian commitment. He was, however, a marked man from that point onwards, and several people in the church were simply waiting for an excuse to accuse him of some kind of inappropriate behaviour.

The whole issue came to a head during a special youth evening that was organized at the church. James was his usual self, loud and jocular, the heart and soul of the party. Those who liked him thought that this was great; those who didn't like him found him to be his usual discourteous self. As the night wore on, an argument broke out between James and one of the girls in the youth fellowship. It was a stupid argument that began needlessly, and both were to blame. The argument became heated, with the girl saying some pretty nasty things to James and him ridiculing her in his usual hilarious way. Then he went one step too far and swore at her. He only meant it as a joke and genuinely did not intend to be offensive; it was just one of those occasions when his big mouth and overly zealous sense of humour took over. For a moment, he thought of apologizing, but then just laughed the whole thing off.

The matter did not end there. The girl, her boyfriend and one of her other friends, all of whom disliked James, reported what he had said to one of the elders. The elder felt the need to take immediate action. He was wise enough to recognize that both parties bore equal responsibility for the incident, but, given James's reputation and the prejudice that most people felt towards him, any action taken was bound to run the risk of being somewhat reactionary. The elder phoned James up and told him sternly that he was coming round to speak to him. James, who lacked subtlety, still considered the whole thing to be a bit of a joke, though he apologized on the phone and was quite willing to apologize to the girl herself for what he had said. When he met with this elder, he was aghast to find that he was going to be banned from taking part in communion for a defined period of time and was asked to step down from any responsibility which he had in the youth fellowship.

All of this occurred some years before the time of writing, yet James has never really recovered from what was said to him and the swiftness with which discipline was applied. Swearing, of course, is wrong, even in jest. However, James could not help but feel that discipline was applied not so much because of what he did but because of who he was. He was someone whose face did not fit, and because of this he suffered. Other young people had done worse, yet were not disciplined. In this situation, James would certainly have responded positively had someone just had a word in his ear. Indeed, those who worked with him found him open to correction and even appreciative of it. But the pettiness with which discipline was applied was destructive and unhelpful.

The problem of sloth

The last story involves Geraldine, a woman in her forties. She was the first member of her family to become a Christian but, in time, both her husband and her two children trusted Christ.

She was greatly appreciated by many people within her church, not least because she was a hard worker and was willing to be involved in a number of areas of church life. The difficulty, however, was that Geraldine had a real problem with her attitude towards others.

This issue was observed and identified some time after she joined the church. She was a fairly dour woman and often appeared to be grumpy. Most people simply put it down to her difficult background and lack of spiritual maturity and therefore excused it. As the weeks turned into months and then years, no discernable change or development was noted. It became more and more difficult to blame her spiritual immaturity for her behaviour and she had every opportunity and lots of time to change.

The problem was more than just grumpiness, however. Geraldine was also very critical of some people within the church. If there was someone she did not like, that person soon found out about it. Her sharp tongue and cutting remarks would leave no doubt as to her feelings about him or her. No one ever confronted Geraldine about any of this. Some did not want to discourage her, especially as members of her family were showing an interest in church and becoming Christians. Others were simply afraid of having a confrontation with someone so volatile. The pastor fell into both of these categories. He just wanted to keep the peace, and hoped that, eventually, the Holy Spirit would sort out the problem by changing Geraldine. He often preached about the sins of the tongue, but never actually spoke to Geraldine face to face.

It was at this point that things really went downhill. Several new people joined the church and this brought life and vitality. They were all younger than Geraldine, better educated and more articulate, and this gave her reason to dislike them with considerable vigour. She began to malign them, quietly at first, and then more publicly. As time went on, her criticisms of them became not only strident but blatantly unfair. The pastor became concerned about this and her attitude became the subject of much discussion at leadership meetings. But, rather than do anything, he just prayed that God would deal with her.

None of this had any impact and her slanderous comments continued. Finally, the pastor decided to say something to Geraldine. Rather than going to visit her, however, he waited for an appropriate moment to say something. That moment came three weeks later, when Geraldine made a very insulting remark to someone during the coffee break between church services. The pastor overheard the comment, leaned over and weakly said, 'That was a bit harsh.' When the reply 'I don't care' came back, he simply shrugged his shoulders and retreated with a despairing look and a shake of his head.

The next Sunday, the pastor began a series of sermons on James, and when he got to chapter 3, he made a big point of condemning the sins of the tongue. Everyone recognized the need for a sermon like this, but the pastor delivered it with such uncharacteristic forthrightness that the whole congregation listened intently. Many felt convicted by the sermon but also felt that the word was more appropriate for Geraldine than for most, and they wondered why the pastor had never confronted her personally on the issue— indeed, why she had never been disciplined for the hurt she was clearly causing. Ironically, the one person who felt no sense of conviction was Geraldine herself; by this stage, she was so accustomed to speaking about and to people in whatever way she liked.

Eventually, the whole situation exploded. The sermons on James did nothing to change Geraldine and quite a few people in the church not only were deeply hurt by her comments, but also had lost any sense of confidence in the pastor. Geraldine came to church one day in a particularly foul mood. During the coffee break between the first service and the family service, she had a blazing row with another woman and made some very rude and hurtful remarks, leaving the other woman in tears. The pastor felt that he had to act. He decided to visit Geraldine and speak to her sternly for her behaviour. He also decided that, if she did not apologize, he would take the matter further. However, it was a case of too little too late. The damage had already been done over the years.

This kind of situation is singularly unfortunate because it is so needless. In the same way that a snowball grows and gains momentum as it rolls down a hill, so problems in church life can grow and become enormous if they are not dealt with. The secret is to nip them in the bud. If the pastor had been firm with Geraldine at the very start, this problem could have been sorted out. What is more, the fact that the problem had been ignored for so long made it very difficult to come in at a late stage and try to do something about it. It was a case of closing the stable door once the proverbial horse had bolted.

Clearly, it is much better to remain vigilant and deal with issues as they arise. This will not guarantee that small issues never become big issues, but it will confront them early and, in many cases, the problems will not worsen and much heartache will have been saved.

In conclusion

If one thing is clear by now, it is that church discipline is a difficult issue fraught with all sorts of complications. This realization should not discourage us from applying church discipline but alert us to the fact that we need to think clearly about how we go about it, for we need the wisdom of Solomon.

We also need to ensure that we are creating the kind of church environment within which people can grow in their faith and become more spiritually mature. This necessitates that we teach our churches well so that people within the church know what God expects of them and recognize the importance of holiness of life. We also need good pastoral care so that people feel affirmed and motivated to live as they should. All of this will help to keep sin out and develop Christians who can withstand temptation and spiritual attack.

When things do go wrong—and they will—we need to be alert and recognize the signs. Church leaders need to have the kind of relationship with their flock that enables them to speak in any situation with credibility and compassion. They need to have the courage to speak out when necessary and the gentleness to advise without causing hurt or offence. But there also needs to be a determination to root out anything that does not bring glory to God, even if this means dealing with a church member decisively and severely. In all of this, the church needs to be united so that there is no breaking of rank, no backtracking and no loss of focus. The whole body of Christ needs to speak with one voice, with strength and compassion, so that anyone who falls can be dealt with and restored to a full relationship with Christ and his church. If we can achieve this, we are on the way to being the Christian community which Christ anticipated.

APPENDIX 1

Determining the spiritual health of your church

These seven questions are based on Chapter 3 (Preventive discipline). Working through them may help you to analyse the spiritual health of your church and see which areas need particular attention as part of preventive discipline. For each question, rate your church on a scale of 1–10 (1 representing 'Not at all', and 10 representing 'Very much'). Are there steps that you can take to help your church improve in specific areas?

1. How responsive are the members of your congregation to Bible teaching?
2. How committed are the members of your congregation to reaching spiritual maturity through a disciplined walk with Christ?
3. To what extent could your congregation be described as a community?
4. To what extent do the members of your congregation see themselves as being accountable to one another?
5. To what extent do the members of your congregation respond to guidance?
6. How open are the members of your congregation in sharing their struggles with one another?
7. To what extent can your church be described as a supportive and encouraging church?

APPENDIX 2

Stages of corrective discipline

This outline summarizes the material given in Chapter 4 (Corrective discipline):

- General offence/personal offence: rebuke in private (Titus 1:13) = a quiet but firm word in the ear.
- Initial correction doesn't work: rebuke in private with witnesses (Matt. 18:16) = interim stage of taking witnesses. Do not yet involve whole church.
- No resolution: public rebuke (1 Tim. 5:19–20) = exact implementation depends on model of church. A last resort when all else has failed.
- Still no repentance: withdrawal of confidence (2 Thes. 3:14–15).
- Final stage: excommunication (1 Cor. 5:9–13) = exclusion from the community.

In all these stages, restoration is the aim. It must be made clear to the offender that he or she will be fully welcomed back following repentance.

FOR FURTHER HELP AND INFORMATION

Books

Donahue, Bill, and Bowman, Guy, *Coaching Life-Changing Small Group Leaders: A Practical Guide for Those who Lead and Shepherd Small Group Leaders* (Grand Rapids, MI: Zondervan, 2006)

Poirier, Alfred, *The Peacemaking Pastor: A Biblical Guide to Resolving Church Conflict* (Grand Rapids, MI: Baker, 2006)

Rowdon, Harold (ed.), *Church Leaders Handbook* (Carlisle: Paternoster, 2002)

——*Serving God's People: Re-thinking Christian Ministry Today* (Carlisle: Paternoster, 2006)

Strauch, Alexander, *Leading with Love* (Colorado Springs, CO: Lewis & Roth, 2006)

Websites

www.bible.org
www.glo-europe.org/leadership.html

Information on the Tilsley College mentoring programme can be obtained at college@glo-europe.org

ENDNOTES

1 Calvin believed that these animal skins were a reminder to Adam of his vileness (John Calvin, *Genesis* (Geneva Series of Commentaries; Edinburgh: Banner of Truth, 1984), p. 182). Leupold adds, 'God does provide, for the proper clothing for man's body does suggest and does render reasonable the conclusion that He will provide for the proper covering of man's guilty soul' (H. C. Leupold, *Exposition of Genesis*, vol. 1 (Grand Rapid, MI: Baker Book House, 1987), pp. 78–79).

2 Wenham makes the point that Noah's righteous behaviour and his post-flood sacrifice were evidence of a pre-existing covenant with God (Gordon J. Wenham, *Genesis 1–15* (Word Biblical Commentary; Dallas: Word, 1991), p. 206). The rainbow was also evidence that God's covenant with Noah was then extended to all mankind. The world now had a new beginning and Noah, like Adam, was to be fruitful and fill the earth (Gen. 9:1; compare 1:28).

3 Neil Summerton, *A Noble Task: Eldership and Ministry in the Local Church* (Carlisle: Paternoster Press, 2003), p. 59.

4 Thomas C. Oden, *Pastoral Theology: Essentials of Ministry* (San Francisco: Harper Collins, 1983), p. 189.

ABOUT DAY ONE:

Day One's threefold commitment:
- To be faithful to the Bible, God's inerrant, infallible Word;
- To be relevant to our modern generation;
- To be excellent in our publication standards.

I continue to be thankful for the publications of Day One. They are biblical; they have sound theology; and they are relevant to the issues at hand. The material is condensed and manageable while, at the same time, being complete—a challenging balance to find. We are happy in our ministry to make use of these excellent publications.

JOHN MACARTHUR, PASTOR-TEACHER, GRACE COMMUNITY CHURCH, CALIFORNIA

It is a great encouragement to see Day One making such excellent progress. Their publications are always biblical, accessible and attractively produced, with no compromise on quality. Long may their progress continue and increase!

JOHN BLANCHARD, AUTHOR, EVANGELIST AND APOLOGIST

Visit our web site for more information and
to request a free catalogue of our books.
www.dayone.co.uk